WHAT
LOVE
LOOKS
LIKE

WHAT **LOVE** LOOKS LIKE

12 LEADERS TELL WHEN LOVE BROKE THROUGH THEIR DARKEST MOMENTS

— COMPILED BY —

JAMES W. GOLL

Chosen

a division of Baker Publishing Group
Minneapolis, Minnesota

© 2015 by James W. Goll

Published by Chosen Books
11400 Hampshire Avenue South
Bloomington, Minnesota 55438
www.chosenbooks.com

Chosen Books is a division of
Baker Publishing Group, Grand Rapids, Michigan

Printed in the United States of America

Library of Congress Cataloging-in-Publication Data

Goll, Jim W.
    What love looks like : 12 leaders tell when love broke through their darkest moments / compiled by James W. Goll.
        pages cm
    Summary: "Be inspired by the true stories of twelve Christian leaders who are serving as willing vessels of God's love in our world. Will you follow their lead?"— Provided by publisher.
        ISBN 978-0-8007-9774-4 (pbk. : alk. paper) 1. God (Christianity)—Love. 2. Love—Religious aspects—Christianity. I. Title.
    BT140.G65 2015
    231'.6—dc23   2015005499

Scripture quotations identified NASB are from the New American Standard Bible®, copyright © 1960, 1962, 1963, 1968, 1971, 1972, 1973, 1975, 1977, 1995 by The Lockman Foundation. Used by permission.

Scripture quotations identified NIV are from the Holy Bible, New International Version®. NIV®. Copyright © 1973, 1978, 1984, 2011 by Biblica, Inc.™ Used by permission of Zondervan. All rights reserved worldwide. www.zondervan.com

Scripture quotations identified NKJV are from the New King James Version. Copyright © 1982 by Thomas Nelson, Inc. Used by permission. All rights reserved.

Scripture quotations identified NLT are from the *Holy Bible*, New Living Translation, copyright © 1996, 2004, 2007 by Tyndale House Foundation. Used by permission of Tyndale House Publishers, Inc., Carol Stream, Illinois 60188. All rights reserved.

Scripture quotations identified KJV are from the King James Version of the Bible.

Cover design by LOOK Design Studio

15   16   17   18   19   20   21   7   6   5   4   3   2   1

With a heart of gratitude, I want to dedicate this book to the memory, lineage and legacy of my late wife, Michal Ann Goll, who proceeded to heaven in the fall of 2008. She lived this message. She embodied these truths. She exuded a life of unconditional love. It is my great honor to dedicate this transparent book in honor of Michal Ann Goll and her work with Compassion Acts, a ministry that continues worldwide to this day.

Contents

Contents

Foreword

By Bill Johnson

I love books about radical faith, great achievements and unusual conquests. I absolutely love being provoked by the kind of messages that launch me beyond the boundaries of what has become common. I also love the *behind-the-scenes* stories of people who live on the constant edge of what is thought to be impossible. It feels as though they are summoning me into pursuing things in God I had never even dreamed of. These messages awaken something in me that truly makes me feel alive at a whole new level.

And while *What Love Looks Like* is a summons from God to all that I just mentioned, it will hit the reader at a much deeper place than one might imagine at first glance. Instead of problems, assignments and mission being our conquest, somehow we as the readers become the conquest. And as we become the conquest of God, we learn firsthand the expression of this priceless commodity called *love*. This kind of love is the rarest of all, as it is given away, needing nothing in return to keep it alive.

Let's face it. It is fairly easy to love the lovely, the heroic and those who loved us first. When people celebrate and compliment you, it is always easier to celebrate and compliment them in return. These kinds of relationships are good and are truly gifts from God. But success on that level is not really that noble. Even those who do not know Christ can succeed there. This book brings a much deeper challenge, as it will provoke, inspire and educate the reader on what God's love really looks like. This kind of love is the greatest threat to the powers of darkness, as it is potentially the greatest force in shaping world history. And in the measure we truly receive this love, we are equipped to give it away.

The following pages are filled with the journeys of some of our greatest present-day heroes of the faith. Most of these authors are deep personal friends whom I have been able to watch as their stories first became etched in stone by the love and grace of God. I can testify: They know. They really, really know what love looks like. Each chapter is a true love story. But not in the way you might think. The writers bare their souls as they talk about the parts of their personal journey that are seldom broadcast or written about. In fact, it is much too personal to randomly discuss what is talked about here, lest these priceless experiences become abused through familiarity. Yet here it is—this book is one of those rare treasures. It is as though the Holy Spirit mined the gold from the deep places of these writers' hearts so that each of us might become richer simply by reading. And richer you will be.

Be ready for a new high-water mark in this most precious of all subjects. It remains true—*the greatest of these is love*. Get ready for a summons from God. Be ready for great personal change, as He empowers everyone He summons.

Bill Johnson
Bethel Church, Redding, California
Author, *When Heaven Invades Earth* and *Experience the Impossible*

Foreword

By Randy Clark

James Goll has been used by God to bring forth an amazing book, one that touches our emotions and builds our faith. Along with authoring a chapter, James compiled this book, *What Love Looks Like*, in which twelve key leaders of the Church today give us an honest perspective on life's toughest battles. Most of these leaders I consider personal friends. Others I have met, and a couple of them are new to me. I feel privileged to look inside their stories of the darkest times in their lives and see how God brought them through these seasons.

These amazing, interesting, touching and inspiring stories are the experiences of pastors and co-pastors, itinerant ministers, prophets and missionaries. But they are the kind of experiences all of us could face—the kind common to our humanity. If you want to know how to face life's hardest issues and come out victorious, or if you are going through a hard time yourself right now, you will find hope and a basis for sustained faith in these pages.

Your dark night of the soul may be caused by the accusations and misunderstanding of friends who have turned against you; the loss of your health and your experience of great physical and emotional pain; an accusation of heresy or of being deceived; the grief of losing your spouse; the surprise of the secret immoral life of your mate, who leaves you for a gay lifestyle; your own mortality and what looks like impending death from an incurable disease; or the emotional roller coaster of having hope deferred, which makes your heart sick with disappointment and emotional loss. Whatever the cause, this book will speak hope to you, raise your faith and remind you of how God works good out of all things. James's work will inspire you to remain faithful and finish the race.

This book is not a how-to book. It is neither simplistic, nor an invitation to accept Jesus so you can move forward without any problems. Rather, it is a book that addresses the deepest questions of life, suggesting a way through the valley to the mountain, through the darkness to the light, through hopelessness to hope, through doubt to faith, through bitterness to forgiveness and joy.

I highly recommend *What Love Looks Like*, its compiler and its contributors to you. May you be as blessed as I was in gaining wisdom from those who have faced the vicious situations we sometimes have to face in life and who have come out victorious.

Randy Clark
Founder and president, Global Awakening and the
Apostolic Network of Global Awakening

Acknowledgments

Publishing a book is always a team effort—especially when it comes to publishing a book of this nature, in which we compiled twelve distinct voices into one hopefully cohesive read. That alone was quite an undertaking. But this book comes from an inspiration, and that inspiration has a background.

With this in mind, I first want to acknowledge that the vision of this book had its origin in the Women on the Frontlines conferences, which my late wife, Michal Ann Goll, and I originally hosted. In 2014, I officially turned the leadership reins of this global movement over to my dear friend and champion in the faith, Patricia King. At a series of conference luncheons, Patricia had each of the primary speakers share "their darkest moments" and how love had the final say. Thus the inspiration was cast, and Jane Campbell of Chosen Books and I in turn picked up the baton to put feet to the vision. Mercy, what a task!

So my first act of gratitude goes to the Holy Spirit Himself for His amazing work of inspiration. Second, I want to acknowledge the leadership gift that rests upon Patricia King. She inspires many to be all that they can be in Christ Jesus.

Third, I want to thank the Lord for the mentorship and grace that rest upon Jane Campbell of Chosen Books and the team of editors, artists, promotions people and administration at Baker Publishing Group. They are a company of extreme integrity.

Finally, I want to acknowledge the efforts of each of these Christlike authors. They are all busy in their own sphere of life and ministry, but they sacrificed their personal time to tell their story and trust me with the stewardship of shaping it into *What Love Looks Like: 12 Leaders Tell When Love Broke Through Their Darkest Moments*. Thank you, each and every one, for making this a book unlike anything ever done before!

Introduction

By James W. Goll

Personally, I am ecstatic concerning this book, *What Love Looks Like*. What a novel idea to compile a book on love. Not just any love—but the *agape* kind of love that transcends rational thinking and human love alone. To bring together twelve leaders willing to share their hardships vulnerably, and then to watch how God met each of them in a personal way, is unprecedented.

This project came about as an overflow from an annual Women on the Frontlines conference, where a group of leaders became unusually transparent and told stories from their lives of times when love broke through their darkest moments. Most of us were in tears as we listened. You might be in tears also when you read these gut-wrenching stories.

What Love Looks Like contains true-life stories, mingled with the wisdom of lessons learned and salted with some scriptural teaching. You might end up having your own heart encounter along the way as you read it. This book offers hope. I wept as

I read these chapters from national and international leaders of stature—some of whom I have been an intimate friend with for over 35 years.

This book is unique. It is a charitable book. The royalties are being split equally between two ministries: Iris Ministries, established by Rolland and Heidi Baker, and Compassion Acts, founded by my late wife, Michal Ann Goll. What an honor to bring modern-day champions of the faith together from across a wide and diverse expression of the Body of Christ, toward the common goal of making a difference for Jesus Christ's sake.

So pull up your easy chair, sit back and get out some tissues. This book will change you. It could help start a needed Jesus love revolution in the Church today. Have you learned to love from the heart?

Broken and yet grateful,

James W. Goll
Compiling editor

1

Learning to Love

By Stacey Campbell

If you love Me, you will keep My commandments.

John 14:15 NASB

I sat there, stunned. Surrounded by our friends and co-workers, my husband, Wesley, and I heard their words, but were incredulous at what they were saying.

"We all want you to resign. Here's the paper for you to sign."

These friends and co-workers, some of whom I had walked with for over twenty years, were rejecting me wholesale.

"Just sign the paper and we will make the public announcement this week."

The following week was anguish. I thought of everything God had ever spoken to me about this place. About all the dreams we had seen come true in the last 22 years since we founded the church. I thought about my children and the devastating impact it would have on them to be thrust forcibly from the only spiritual home they had ever had. They were born and raised, dedicated and baptized with these people. And in one week, it was over. Brother against brother. Wounded in the house of friends.

In the weeks that followed, I watched the camps form. I overheard my children's teenage friends saying, "I'm never going back to that place after what they did to you." I saw bitter roots all around me, even in my own heart. And everywhere, the roots were producing fruits. Division was rampant.

The shot was heard around the world. People were calling to ask, "What did you do that was so bad that they fired you?"

Explanation after explanation, recounting the painful story over and over, like a bad record. I watched people around me move into despair, hopelessness and disillusionment. It was intensely painful because it affected not just me. It affected all those closest to me in really significant ways.

Where was God? How could people say, "God told us to do this"? There were questions I could not answer. And questions I could not face.

So I did what was my custom; I turned to find God the way I had always found Him, in good times and bad. I took out my Bible and began to read it, to pray it, to find help in my time of trouble. God always appears to me whenever I do this—in my mountaintop experiences and in my valleys. I hear Him speaking to me through His Word, no matter what my circumstances. This time was no different. I went to the book of Job and began to pray it verse by verse.

Lessons from Job

I love the book of Job. I remember that the first time I read it, I was amazed at how God looked at Job. God was so proud of

him, so confident in Job's heart, that He was not afraid to let
Satan test Job at every level.

God even boasted about Job to the angels: "Have you considered My servant Job? For there is no one like him on the
earth" (Job 1:8; 2:3 NASB).

I marveled that there was a man from whom God received so
much pleasure. And now I had a small opportunity to give God
pleasure, too. I felt the invitation in every verse I read. Sadly, I
was too immature to really do what Job did. Instead of respond-
ing with assurance in God, I harbored anger toward those who
had hurt me. I was indignant at the perceived injustice of it all.

Yet the story of Job confronted me verse after verse. Job
passed every test, no matter how difficult it was. First he lost his
possessions, then his children, and then his wife accused him.
Finally, he lost his health. Sitting there in the dirt with sores all
over his body, he was surrounded by old "friends" who picked
away at his integrity.

What amazes me about Job is that he just sat there and
took it, for the most part. Jesus, our perfect example, was even
stronger in His weakness. He would not open His mouth when
accused. He stood like a lamb before His shearers, and then, as
they jeered and tortured Him, He said, "Father, forgive them,
for they don't know what they are doing" (Luke 23:34 NLT).

I do not know how Jesus could say that. When I read the
story of the crucifixion, it seems to me that they knew exactly
what they were doing and killed Him on purpose, and that
Jesus plainly spoke to them about what they would do before
they did it.

Yet it was in my search for the heart of God through the words
of Scripture that He began to show me that even suffering and
injustice have meaning and purpose. Studying Job and Jesus
helped me during this painful time when all my relationships
were being blown apart. I was able to find the deeper place in the

heart of God, to go beyond the obvious pain to the fellowship of His sufferings. If I did not want bitterness and unforgiveness to overcome me, I was going to have to find God in this valley, because there would be no miraculous turnaround.

Perhaps the whole situation was an invitation, an answer to many of my previous prayers to know God in every way He could be known (see Philippians 3:10). Perhaps it was an "aha!" moment where I could see how I had also hurt people and cut them off as though I did not need them. Perhaps it was an opening into the mystery of the oneness of His Body and how deeply it cuts when division is active. Perhaps God wanted me to learn to love the way He does, by loving not only those who are like me and who agree with and support me, but even loving those who hurt me. Perhaps He was giving me a fuller Gospel, and with it the ability to bless and not curse. Perhaps? I think that was it.

What a Patient Father God

I wish I could say I passed that test and excelled at the opportunity it gave me. The reality was that I failed miserably. I was mad. I was indignant. I was defensive and responded with equal amounts of accusation of my own. But the good news is that when we fail, we get to try again. We are never doomed to live in our past failures. We are always given a second, a third, a seventy-times-seventieth chance. What a patient Father.

And so it was that over time, through much prayer and with the incredible support of another church family in our same little town in British Columbia (they hired us on their staff and kept encouraging us), we got our second chance. Four years later, through a series of extraordinary events, we began to meet with the very friends who had fired us. It began on the rugby field, with one of the elders who had terminated us. After seeing us, he then set up meetings with the leadership team of the church. One by one, we began to meet with them in dozens of face-to-face meetings.

Of course, it was not easy. We had 85 meetings before we could go back to our home church and stand together with the elders who had fired us. Both Wesley and I and the elders repented to the Body for our mutual inability to work through the issues that had divided us.

Think of it . . . 85 meetings just to restore enough trust to stand together and give a unified message. Then another 65 meetings to get to the place where we were invited back into leadership. It seemed that everyone—both those who had left after the painful incident and those who had stayed—were hurt. But we did come together again. People everywhere rejoiced. Why? Because love won!

We all know that church splits usually do not end well. Animosity seems to last a lifetime. But the Bible tells us to go to our brother when we are divided (see Matthew 18:15–17). Disagreements will come. They come to everyone—families, workmates, churches. Wherever there are people, there sometimes will be disagreements. The issue is not in keeping stumbling blocks from coming. They will surely come (see Matthew 18:7). The issue is how we handle them. Paul and Peter disagreed on doctrine. But they disagreed face-to-face, not behind each other's backs (see Galatians 2:11). They did not each set up camp and tell one side of the story. They sat together and laid out their arguments.

I have discovered that there is no substitute for the face-to-face. I have also learned that when you stay in the room, you can overcome almost anything. Those who leave the room—though they may move on—often cannot overcome the things they harbored at the point when they left the room. It is in the perpetual practice of three things—the ongoing rub of "iron sharpening iron" (see Proverbs 27:17), the long-term learning of another's point of view and the living of the slow-to-judge lifestyle—that we really learn to love.

Did You Learn How to Love?

When I think of learning to love, I often recall a life-and-death experience of a wonderful prophetic father who has greatly influenced many of us. Bob Jones was a simple prophet from the backwoods of Arkansas, but his experiences with God were profound. The story I remember happened in August 1975, when the Lord appeared to Bob as a ball of light.

Bob recounted, "It was like a ball of light that came toward me. My eyes were wide open, and the Spirit spoke out of the light and told me that I should prophesy against abortion. God had never done that to me before."

Bob was excited, and he began to do as he was commanded. Then a strange thing happened. A demonic spirit appeared and told Bob that if he would not prophesy against abortion and the coming homosexual agenda, then he would receive fame, fortune and everything he wanted. But if he did prophesy as he was told, then the spirits of darkness would kill him.

Bob flatly refused the offer: "I rose up and said, 'In the name of Jesus, you can't touch me, and I will do the will of God.'"

The next day, August 8, 1975, Bob again prophesied against abortion. About thirty minutes after prophesying, however, he suddenly became sick to his stomach and felt pain in various parts of his body. His stomach became hard as a rock. He began hemorrhaging out of his mouth and nose. Blood began to squirt out so fast that he was bleeding to death.

"I had no idea what was happening," he said. "I was in so much pain."

His wife rushed him to the hospital, but the doctors were mystified. Knowing that this was a spiritual attack, Bob asked that he be taken home—to pray. As Bob lay there on his bed, suffering immense pain, his spirit struggled to stay in his body. In a single moment, he felt his spirit disconnect from his body and float to the ceiling.

Confused, Bob wondered, *How can this happen? How can a demonic spirit actually take my life while I am doing God's will?*

The next thing Bob knew, he was in paradise. All he could feel was pure love, pure joy and the power of God. Even though he was aware that his body was lying on the bed below, Bob knew he was somewhere in a heavenly place. Bob saw Jesus and moved toward Him. As he did so, he became aware that he was seeing the departed spirits of those who had just died from all over the world as they also approached Jesus. As Bob began to focus on Jesus, he became conscious of a long line of people on a moving conveyer belt who were being brought closer and closer to Jesus. All of them were coming to stand before the Lord.

As each person came before Him, Jesus would ask only one question: "Did you learn how to love?"

Bob said he saw all ages and types of people. Some had been afflicted with crippling diseases while on earth. People were there from every walk of life. And each one was asked that same question: "Did you learn how to love?"

After people responded to the question, Jesus would then kiss them on the lips and they would go through the great big double doors of His heart, into paradise.

Bob said he especially noticed one older lady whom he somehow knew had become bitter and mean from the hardships of her life. Again Jesus asked, "Did you learn how to love?"

She answered, "Only You, Lord . . . only You!"

She went in, but it seemed as if she had no reward.

Finally, Bob himself came before Jesus. Jesus held up His hand and said, "Wait, Bob . . . it's not your time. You died doing My will on earth. It's not your time to be here."

Because of the wonderful presence of God all around him, Bob did not want to go back. He protested and asked to stay. But God sent him back to earth with that one question ringing in his ears: "Did you learn how to love?"

Though this experience happened many years ago, I find myself thinking of it often. Bob lived for another forty years before he finally went on to his reward, graduating on Valentine's Day, 2014. But the penetrating question that will be asked of us all remains: "Did you learn how to love?" Every time I face relational tensions, the question comes back to me: "Stacey, did you learn how to love?"

The Lifestyle Example of Jesus

Bob Jones's life-and-death experience hammers home the example Jesus gave us in word and deed during His time on earth. So often, I am confronted by the words of Scripture, especially by the second commandment Jesus gave us: "Love your neighbor as yourself" (Matthew 22:39 NASB). In particular, I am confronted by the fact that Jesus repeatedly measures how we are doing at His first commandment—to love Him with all our heart, soul, strength and mind—by how we are doing at the second commandment. Jesus is so absolutely in love with humanity that He asks us to express our love for Him by loving one another. When we see a poor person, we are to treat him or her as we would treat Jesus (see Matthew 25:34–46). When we go to worship, we are first to make sure we have no division with our brothers (see Matthew 5:23–24).

If we truly love God, then we are to demonstrate it first and foremost by how we treat one another. God insists that living in love with our brothers on earth is an essential part of loving Him:

Beloved, let us love one another, for love is from God; and everyone who loves is born of God and knows God. The one who does not love does not know God, for God is love. . . . Beloved, if God so loved us, we also ought to love one another.

1 John 4:7–8, 11 NASB

We love, because He first loved us. If someone says, "I love God," and hates his brother, he is a liar; for the one who does not love his brother whom he has seen, cannot love God whom he has not seen. And this commandment we have from Him, that the one who loves God should love his brother also.

1 John 4:19–21 NASB

God is love. And love gives. Because He is love, He desires that we love, too. God is the least egocentric Person I have ever met. The more I study Him, the more I learn His ways, the more I understand that our worship of God looks like loving others. Certain Scriptures have led me to believe this: Because love is at the core of who God is, and because love is expressed in giving to another person, then possibly the greatest way God wants us to show our love for Him is by following Jesus' second commandment.

A new commandment I give to you, that you love one another, even as I have loved you, that you also love one another. By this all men will know that you are My disciples, if you have love for one another.

John 13:34–35 NASB

He who has My commandments and keeps them is the one who loves Me; and he who loves Me will be loved by My Father, and I will love him and will disclose Myself to him. . . . If anyone loves Me, he will keep My word; and My Father will love him, and We will come to him and make Our abode with him. He who does not love Me does not keep My words; and the word which you hear is not Mine, but the Father's who sent Me.

John 14:21, 23–24 NASB

If you keep My commandments, you will abide in My love; just as I have kept My Father's commandments and abide in His love.

John 15:10 NASB

This is My commandment, that you love one another, just as I have loved you. Greater love has no one than this, that one lay down his life for his friends. You are My friends if you do what I command you. . . . This I command you, that you love one another.

John 15:12–14, 17 NASB

The entire earthly life of Jesus modeled unconditional love. He went to His own people and loved them even when they rejected Him. He washed His disciples' feet and said,

Do you know what I have done to you? You call me Teacher and Lord; and you are right, for so I am. If I then, the Lord and the Teacher, washed your feet, you also ought to wash one another's feet. For I gave you an example that you also should do as I did to you.

John 13:13–15 NASB

The Supreme Example of Love

So what does love look like? Love looks like patience, kindness, long-suffering. Love looks like bearing a lot of "stuff" and believing all the things God wants us to believe, even in the face of violent opposition. Love looks like those iconic faces of love and forgiveness and endurance—Mother Teresa, Nelson Mandela, Elie Wiesel. And sometimes love looks like you and me—struggling along in the trenches of time, trying to behold the Supreme Example of love, till we are ever-increasingly transformed, promise by promise, partaking of His divine nature, simply because, like Job, we want to give Him pleasure. He is just so beautiful, so lovely. And He calls us to look like Him by looking at Him (see 2 Corinthians 3:18).

All of us will experience hard times. I have dear friends who have endured way more difficult things than I have. Through their hard times, they have shown me what love looks like. Many of these friends are not well-known on earth, but they give God pleasure. I know He is proud of them.

And so it was that four years after our failure, after countless face-to-face meetings, we all humbled ourselves—working through love, forgiveness and reconciliation—till we were united. We were invited back into the same church. We began to serve together on the same leadership team. We experienced a unity victory. And we somehow love each other now more than we ever did before.

What does love look like to me? Love bears all things, love believes all things, love hopes all things . . . and love wins! I have set as my aim learning how to love. What about you?

Learning to love,
Stacey Campbell

Stacey and Wesley Campbell founded RevivalNOW! Ministries and a mercy organization for children at risk called Be A Hero. They also serve on staff at New Life Church in Kelowna. Information about their ministries is available at http://revivalnow.com and http://www.beahero.org.

2

A Walking Dead Man

By James Maloney

For you have died and your life is hidden with Christ in God.

Colossians 3:3 NASB

I remember being locked in a closet as a toddler. With nothing but a bottle of water, lying on the floor, looking out through the crack at the bottom of the door, crying myself hoarse, desperate for that last little sliver of light before the sun set and I was plunged into suffocating darkness. I was still in the same soiled, wool blanket that served as a diaper, which created terrible sores and welts. As that light disappeared, I would scream and scream and scream, and no one would come rescue me. No one. I was utterly alone in pitch blackness, an unwanted and unloved baby, cast away, a nuisance who would not shut up. For days at a time I was locked away alone, and this did not happen just once or twice.

I was maybe two or three, and this is my earliest memory. Other children probably remember their birthday presents, bright balloons and a cake. They probably have some warm memory of a mother's gentle caress, a father's kind words and a smile. Perhaps those memories include a puppy dog, a doll, a toy car. I just remember that dark closet. That crushing, aching, longing feeling in the pit of my hungry, empty stomach: alienation, isolation, rejection. And fear. Smothering, black fear. It hurt so badly, that ache of emptiness. Even then I knew I was unwanted, and it crippled me for years and years to come. No one should know what that feels like, let alone a child.

Not What Love Looks Like

I do not think my mother was actively trying to kill me. She was just a teenager whose husband had been incarcerated. Left to her own meager devices, she did not have the food to feed me. During her husband's stint in jail, she turned to a Christian minister for counseling. They had an affair, and she illegitimately conceived yours truly. Trust me when I say I come from humble beginnings.

But when my mother's husband was paroled, he came home and saw me sitting on the floor, this toddler who he knew could not be his, and he *did* try to kill me.

Flying in a demonic rage across the room, he stomped down on my face with his boot and disfigured my features, crushing a section of the orbital bone at the bridge of my nose, mangling my ear. He picked me up by the ankles and slammed me into the wall over and over.

It was the supernatural protection of the Lord, and nothing else, that spared my life during the months of torment that followed. My mother ended up locking me in the closet in a weird attempt to protect me from her husband's wrath. Odd way of thinking, I know. Thankfully, my adoptive parents showed enough love and compassion to get the authorities to step in. They stormed into the house, broke down the closet door and pulled me out of a situation that undoubtedly would have resulted in my death before my fourth birthday.

But always with me were that closet and the fading light, those feelings of loneliness and nonacceptance, the black icy fear of being cast off. Those feelings were worse than the pain of physical abuse.

I lack the space to elaborate in depth on my childhood, and I have recorded my testimony elsewhere. But for my purpose here, I needed to outline some of the horrors I experienced as a small child. Those incidents play a huge role in the revelation the Father gave me that I want to share with you. In telling you these things, I am endeavoring to further unveil the Father's heart of love toward us. Even in the midst of difficult circumstances and the testing of our faith, God's love is never rescinded. We all *know* this, or at least we give it some sort of mental assent. "God's banner of love over me is unconditional," we say (see Song of Solomon 2:4). But it is the expression of that love during our darkest moments that many times spiritually proves what we mentally know.

Just as God's righteousness and justice are incapable of changing, so is His love. There cannot be one without the other in equal measure, perfectly balanced. "Righteousness and justice are the foundation of Your throne; mercy and truth go before Your face," Psalm 89:14 (NKJV) says. "In mercy the throne will be established; and One will sit on it in truth, in the tabernacle of David, judging and seeking justice and hastening righteousness," Isaiah 16:5 (NKJV) says. I recently had an experience that proved all this to me after forty years of full-time ministry.

As wonderful and true as John 3:16 is in telling us that God so loved the world that He sent His only Son, I believe there is a greater continuation of that love for the whole world, in that it does not stop there. It is personalized for each child of God, and it is more fully expressed by Christ's words in John 14:23 (NKJV): "If anyone loves Me, he will keep My word; and My Father will love him, and We will come to him and make Our home with him."

Jesus is speaking in the context of returning to His Father's house, where there are many mansions or dwellings (see John 14:2). He tells us how the Spirit will "abide with you forever . . . for He dwells with you and will be in you" (John 14:16–17 NKJV). We are not orphans, because we love Him: "And he who loves Me will be loved by My Father, and I will love him and manifest Myself to him" (verse 21 NKJV).

Toward a Deeper Understanding

This gives us a deeper understanding of the love God expresses in John 3:16 for the people of the world, which they do not comprehend because the "ruler of this world" (John 14:30 NKJV) has slighted God's character to them. The ruler of this world has implied that God's love does not *abide*, but is conditional and fractured, capable of changing—and they are left with a "peace" as the world gives it (see verse 27). It is a distorted view that claims love is some flitting, cosmic outside force that can shift as the wind blows, not a personal indwelling of God Himself, who is Love, according to 1 John 4:8.

The Lord was talking about establishing an *abode* of love, however, wherein the Triune God Himself "sets up shop" inside you as one of His children. This is what true love looks like, and it can be in our darkest moments that a true revelation of God's heart of love toward us will shine through most brightly.

Not that God *creates* the darkest moments, but He *uses* the circumstances of the so-called "long, dark night of the soul" to shed abroad His love in our hearts through the help of the Holy Spirit (see Romans 5:5), and He also shows His holiness and resolute sense of justice. It all goes hand in hand. His love never changes, but He expects *us* to change around His love.

To me, the greatest purpose of supernatural expression in the form of signs, wonders, miracles and healing is to show the world, and us, the Father's true heart of love. These expressions also cripple the maligning slander of the accuser, who attempts to slur God's character. They are given not just so we can witness a miracle and "ooh and aah," but rather, so that we will see the Love behind that miracle. That is why it saddens me when Christians downplay the release of the miraculous, because it downplays the homestead God is trying to establish inside each of us. An absence of the miraculous can decrease love, and as a once-popular song used to say, what the world needs the most now is love, right?

A Bad Diagnosis

That is where I am coming from. Now let me share with you one of my most recent "darkest moments," which is connected to all I have told you already. In the spring of 2013, I realized one day that I had a lump bulging out of my left eyebrow that hurt like there was no tomorrow. I am a big guy, and I think I have a pretty high pain threshold, but this put me on the floor. I had to cancel meetings, and nothing over-the-counter brought the slightest relief. I went to a wonderful, Spirit-filled dermatologist friend, who biopsied the growth and saw all this scar tissue and peripheral cysts. He said they came from minuscule orbital bone fragments buried deep under the skin where the brow meets the nose, all mashed up with the muscle tissue, where they had been festering for the past five decades or so.

The only contribution of my mother's husband to my life, sadly.

They called what I had a squamous-cell carcinoma (SCC), a slow-growing tumor, the second most common type of skin cancer after basal carcinomas. While it is dangerous, SCC is not as aggressive as melanoma, which is often life-threatening. The biopsy showed this one was not malignant, but still, we are not talking a little freckle here. It was threaded deep in the muscle tissue all the way to the bone. My dermatologist friend performed surgery to remove the tumor and countless peripheral cysts all the way down to the bone, and then he stitched me back up.

While the dermatologist *felt* he got all of it, he suggested I have the margins tested to make sure. The results came back clear, and we thought that was the end of it. I was still experiencing a lot of pain, but I figured it was due to the surgery. Only, as the summer came around, the pain steadily intensified. By late July it had become unbearable. This time it was not just my left eye, but stabbing knives in my head.

My vision became distorted as the pain escalated quickly. I went to a doctor, and he held his finger in front of me, moving it off to my left side. My wife watched in shock as my right eye followed the movement of his finger, while my left eye remained stuck in the middle position. He prescribed hydrocodone for the pain and sent me to an ophthalmologist.

The ophthalmologist ordered a CT scan and discovered a growth on my brain shelf, in the tiny venous cavernous area where the trigeminal nerve enters the brain. He explained that most likely a trauma had occurred to my orbital bone sometime in my life and that cysts had formed, but they had been held at bay by my immune system, possibly for decades.

Suddenly I was a toddler again, back in the black closet, remembering that army boot crushing my face. I remembered my swollen, red fingertips embedded with splinters as I clawed at that closet door, screaming for someone, anyone to let me out. I remembered each and every time some child taunted me about my facial deformities at school.

When I finally underwent plastic surgery as a young adult, I supposed all that had been put to rest. I knew my identity in Christ. I was one of His servant leaders; He had entrusted a fairly well-known (or at least hopefully well-respected) international ministry to me, right? But the enemy brought it all to my remembrance afresh, and I felt utterly alone, isolated once again. It was as if a wave of futility and depression washed over me, and I was buried under an avalanche of frustration. And that never-ending, excruciating pain.

I wanted to climb the walls. Panic. Fear. It all came crashing down on me as I sat in that doctor's office, listening to him explain that the childhood beatings were resurfacing again decades later. Cells from the orbital tumor had moved like a trail of ants along the optic nerve back to the area beneath my brain, and the tumor there was in an inoperable location. Left untreated, it could spread to my brain. The only recourse was radiation.

Of course, I bucked against that. The Lord was my Healer, not radiation. But the pain was intensifying daily, ramping up my fear. I started to withdraw inwardly, alienating myself, feeling depression threaten to swallow me alive. *Where is God in all this?* I asked myself. *Why am I seemingly alone in this ordeal?*

By this point I was eating hydrocodone like candy, so I started on oral morphine and fentanyl patches. The doses climbed higher and higher each week, yet nothing helped. I would lie very still in one position in my dark room, as dark thoughts swirled around my tortured brain. No way to distract myself, no way to watch television with my distorted vision, no way to interact with my family. To top it all off, the tumor was located in close proximity to the appetite control center. Severe nausea was unrelenting, and I lost almost one hundred pounds during the course of the year.

Did God Really Care?

My wife, Joy, faithfully drove me to daily radiation treatments—two, three hours a day on the road in Dallas rush-hour traffic, laying me down in the car, covering my head from the light. I would shuffle slowly into the building as she led me along like a sick, lost child. No, I was like a walking dead man! That is what morphine does to you. Nothing is real; you are trapped in a twilight of false wakefulness, dreaming on your feet. And you cannot escape. You can never escape the phobias of dreamland. I was a living nightmare inside, a shell outside.

In my quiet, dark world of incessant pain and nausea, my mind was racked with questions. *What had opened the door to all this suffering?* Proverbs 26:2 (NKJV) says, "A curse without cause shall not alight." Surely the Lord was aware of what was going on in my body long before I knew about it. *So why hadn't I been healed?* I had spent four decades praying for the sick in my travels and seeing the Lord work so powerfully for thousands of people. It did not seem right that I should suffer so, in light of my entire quest to bring healing to others. I had seen major miracles—metal disappear, tumors vanish and on and on. *Didn't God care?*

Okay, yes, on some level I *knew* He did. But it is hard to focus on His unending love when you are trapped in unending pain and are shutting down emotionally because you feel trapped in a closet. It did not seem right that my stepfather was still inflicting pain on me fifty-some years later. Even though my heavenly Father had revealed His own heart to me when I was fifteen, it seemed as though I again was locked in the closet of isolation and alienation.

I was conscious of nothing else except pain. Nothing else registered—no concept of God's love, of *anyone's* love—just pain. Dozens of times, it took every ounce of willpower not to have my wife take me to the ER so they could just zonk me out. The doctors even told me this pain was a *good* thing, if you can believe that. Ha! They said it was my nerves coming back to life. And yet I still felt like a dead man.

During those months I spent in bed, Satan tried to heap blame and condemnation on me. He accused God's nature to me, attempting to distort the Truth through his lies. Deep depression settled in as my life spiraled downward, completely contrary to everything I had been taught in my Word of Faith background, exacerbated by the murky depths of medication-induced dullness. A walking dead man, indeed. Questions, questions with seemingly no answers, plagued me. I had seen countless thousands of people healed by God's grace alone, and now I suffered under an unbearable yoke of pain, feeling so alone.

How Could This Happen?

My family prayed with such intensity over my bed, rebuking the devil and proclaiming my healing. Joy read the Word to me, holding my hand and speaking life to every cell of my body. Her faith was tenacious and her compassion unending, but still I found no relief. It was as if I had been cut off from the life force of God.

Whenever morphine could induce an hour of sleep for me, my wife would leave my bedside and walk under the stars, begging the Lord to lift this hideous torment. She pleaded with Him to remove it no matter what the cost, yet the torture continued. Joy would tell God, "I don't care if we go further in Your purposes and plans—just take this pain out of my husband's body."

But to put it bluntly, it seemed as if God said and did nothing in reply.

At times the pain was so evil, I would try pacing the floor, as if trying to run away from myself, often staggering and falling. Praying out loud was too painful, so I whispered in tongues for hours each day—it was all I could do. One night I had been pacing for several hours straight when a striking blow to my head made me feel as though I had suffered a gunshot. It threw me to my knees, but somehow I was able to crawl to the couch.

I cried out, "God, I can't hear from You!"

Suddenly, I felt my spirit being lifted up and up and up. I found myself in the Father's throne room, away from the pain, kneeling at a golden railing with pillars on either side. I heard cries of worship rising up from below the throne, and clouds of unapproachable light overwhelmed me. I was incapable of looking up, so I did not see the Father Himself. I did hear Him audibly speak in a commanding, yet reassuring, voice.

Not addressing my pain, He asked only, "Will you go where I tell you to go? Will you say what I tell you to say? Will you do what I tell you to do?"

I answered with an abandoned, "Yes, Lord!"

He merely stated, "You must walk in a greater level of My holiness if you are to go higher in My purposes."

Then I was back in my pain-ridden body.

So there I was, a wall in front of my face, and I was not going to progress in His purposes without dealing with certain issues in my life. When busyness is gone and time is all you have, it is amazing how the Holy Spirit can show you to yourself. I began admitting to things He showed me. He pinpointed strongholds in my mind—frustrations with the Body of Christ, even resentments I had not let broach the light of day. I had lost a lot of faith in God's people, and I did not believe they really much cared. After giving forty years of my life for them, I basically felt that I had just been used a lot of the time. Ministry was fulfilling, yet it was also a struggle. Someone once told me I was feeling "overworked and underpaid." That was true. I always strove to give 110 percent, and it often felt rather one-sided.

Isaiah 19 pronounces the Lord's judgment against Egypt. How did God set "Egyptians against Egyptians" (verse 2)? He mingled a perverse spirit in their midst (see verse 14). They were destroyed from the inside out by the things they spoke against one another, casting each other's images to the ground. That is literally what a "perverse spirit" is, to tear someone down with words. To a certain extent, I was guilty of this. Maybe I had not vocalized my frustrations externally, but I had dwelt on them internally. The effect is the same.

Not to equate my situation as anywhere near touching Job's, but I think there is a principle here that smacks against the grain of my Word of Faith teaching—but that does not make it any less true. There *are* testings. Satan, from time to time, is required to give an account before the Lord (see Job 1:6). It is quite possible that Job's ordeal was a result of fear and perhaps also his perverse speaking, though this is just my opinion (see Job 3:25–26).

Inspected by the Enemy

It is my humble conviction that all ministers—but specifically, prophets and seers—are on occasion (though not every moment of every day) inspected by the enemy, who is looking for hedges that are down (see Ecclesiastes 10:8). And if we are going to increase to the next level in the Lord's glory, these broken hedges must be addressed. In my instance, the open door was verbal condemnation. Frustration about forty years of draining ministry had led me to exhaustion, giving way to anxiety, old phobias and fears. It was like being locked in the closet once again. I had come full circle.

All those phobias—the fear and anxiety, the terrors I had experienced in that closet—translated into exhaustion, anger and frustration in my fifties, leading to this open door that caused the tumor to develop. Through the pain, adversity, fear and depression, the enemy was attempting to shatter my understanding of the Father's heart of love toward me. Satan was trying to deceive me into thinking that God was not speaking, that I was isolated, that I was alienated from the love of God.

In the midst of indescribable pain, my throne room encounter with the Lord proved that His love was manifested toward me no matter what shortcomings I had. Not that it *excused* those shortcomings, but He loved me enough to show them to me. And also to reveal how Satan is bringing a great attack against the people of God, especially among His prophets and seers.

Why? Because these trials can be tools the Lord is allowing that will teach us the importance of dying to ourselves—having this Jordan River experience. The people of God are on the banks of crossing over into the next phase, the next level of His miraculous expression. Great and miraculous expressions of His love will surely come forth from what I call the emerging "Holy Spirit Dove Company" of those on whom His Spirit rests without measure. But we cannot proceed until these "death to self" issues are dealt with.

As these notions rose to the surface, I found myself repenting of attitudes that had gone unchecked. I fell on the Rock, allowing myself to break. I had come to the banks of the Jordan River. This was a type of death experience.

The word *Jordan* means "to go down." And just as Israel could not enter into their inheritance, their promised land, without crossing their own Jordan, we as the people of God must *go down*, too—die to ourselves, leave our Egypt experiences behind us, cut off our ties with the "old man"—both spiritually, as in the way we used to live, and in the natural, as in our ties with the person who has the boot in our faces. We must shut down that perverse spirit and deal with our fears, anxieties and frustrations—our own *closet experiences*. And we all have them.

That is what I mean by death to self. Before we are permitted to cross over, we have to get to a point in God where we leave our personal ambitions drowning in the river. We need to leave behind things like our drive for recognition and our "comeuppance" against those who have done us wrong. Whatever the testing may be, it all must be drowned in the river before we can cross over.

Death to Self—Life for Others!

I am entering my fourth and final phase of ministry. (I call it that based on things the Lord has shown me, but that is a story for another day.) In this final phase, I am looking to receive the full portion of God's blessing, but I cannot enter in without dealing with my present-day closet experience. And the Lord has shown me that neither can any of you. As we each die to our own purposes, even to our own destinies if the Lord wills, we learn yet again that nothing else matters except intimacy with Jesus. Out of that intimacy will flow love for others, which will bring healing in the way He did when He walked this earth. This is what it means for Him to establish an *abode* with us. This is what love looks like.

Through this greatest trial of my life, while the enemy told me the Lord had disappeared, I learned God truly is touched with the feelings of our infirmities (see Hebrews 4:15). I had opened the door through my own shortcomings, and whatever disillusionment it brought, I rediscovered that His love is never far from us. Nor is His demand for holiness (see 1 Peter 1:16). I could not bypass this process at the Jordan. And this, too, is what love looks like.

That throne room experience, in the midst of deepest pain, was the beginning of my restoration. True, the Lord had given me a command. But there was also reassurance. His throne is, indeed, established on justice and mercy—but even in justice God speaks with love. And this is what true love looks like: He used this testing (though He did not author it) to bring me a revelation of His love and faithfulness—something the enemy was trying to destroy.

I had high levels of *faith* for other people to be healed, but I had minimal *trust* in the Lord's reliability and constancy for myself. This was a weak link in my chain that the enemy used against me, but the Lord in His unwavering love (and holiness) called me out on it.

Four Avenues of Love

The Lord showed His love to me in my darkest hour through four avenues. I have already mentioned two—the throne room encounter and how the love of my family undergirded me while I was in the pit.

The third avenue was through the Body of Christ. I experienced the great love of His people through their kind responses, prayers and giving. How amazed I was to discover how much they truly did care! People gave and gave to keep our bills current during the eight months I could not travel in ministry. People prayed and prayed for me—sometimes throughout the night. My mind still reels from the love they poured out. My heart has never been so touched and softened as it was during this trial, when I witnessed the kindness of the saints. Thank you!

The fourth avenue God used to show His love was through a simple seven-pound creature. During the roughest five months, when I lived on very high doses of morphine and fentanyl, I dreaded each day, especially at night, because one side effect of these drugs can be a problem with breathing and suffocation. Our little blond Chihuahua, Fiji, took it upon herself to be my guardian during those months. She positioned herself up against my rib cage day and night, and would not leave her post. Each time my breathing would become erratic, breaking rhythm and coming to a stop, Fiji would crawl up my chest and begin licking my cheek to wake me and get me breathing right again. Big waves of love can flow through a tiny animal!

I resumed traveling again in the spring of 2014, and I am steadily regaining my strength. I am walking through the manifestation of my full healing, believing for a total recovery of my vision. It is not there yet, and I still deal with nearly constant pain, but I am so thankful that I am not reliant on medications any longer. I believe the sickness that has been used as a harness to teach me will be fully dispelled. Complete restoration will be mine, as it was for Job. I am coming out on the other side.

Love is breaking through my understanding and touching my heart like never before. It is not just about the power of God and the release of the Holy Spirit's many gifts; it is ultimately all about receiving and releasing the lasting fragrance of the love of God.

Through it all, I see the plight of humanity and God's eagerness to set people free like never before. He reveals many of their circumstances to me supernaturally as I pray for them. He instills faith, intervenes, and by the finished work of the cross of Jesus, He heals them.

I understand now what they are going through.

And so does Jesus!
James Maloney

James Maloney is an accomplished theologian and well-respected prophetic voice. He is president of Voice of the Dove Company International. Information about his ministry is available at http://www.voiceofthedove company.com.

3

God's Love in the Face of Death

By Heidi Baker

This is how we know what love is: Jesus Christ laid
down his life for us.

1 John 3:16 NIV

One of the darkest times of my life was in 2005, when I
was diagnosed with Methicillin-resistant Staphylococcus aureus (MRSA), a life-threatening staph infection.
When I first came down with this, I ended up in a hospital
in Malaysia. By faith, I checked myself out and returned to
Mozambique, believing I would be healed. The exact opposite
happened, and I became worse. I then headed straight to a
hospital in South Africa.

Many people had faith for my healing and prayed for me while I was hospitalized. Some came in and commanded me to get up in the name of Jesus. I wanted to obey them and do what they said, but I was extremely weak. Even if I could stand up for a couple of minutes, as soon as they left, I would collapse again. It was really hard because I so wanted to be healed, but instead I got weaker and weaker.

Soon after these failed attempts, I pressed in even more for my healing. I declared that I was going to be healed in the name of Jesus. By faith, I decided to check myself out of the hospital and head back to Mozambique. Many of the children and pastors came to the airport to welcome me home. They were singing, dancing and rejoicing. When the children ran up to hug me, I was so weak that I fell down. They were excited and really wanted to see me healed. Even though I was frail, I was determined to press in and not give up.

It's Worth the Price!

Around that same time, we had just started to reach the Makua tribe with the Good News of Christ, and many were coming to Jesus. I preached that Sunday, and around fifty people from the Makondi and Makua tribes got saved. I was excited because I knew that it was worth any price for one soul. At the same time, I had a raging fever and open wounds. I was so ill that it was hard to stand up.

While on my face in the dirt, I remember praying, "God, please heal me, or I am going to die. I must have more of You! I don't want to die of a flesh-eating disease."

My condition continued to deteriorate. My team urged me to return to the hospital in South Africa. The next day, I headed to the airport. The airline workers did not want to let me on the plane because I was so pale that they thought I might die during the flight. I went into the bathroom, put on blush and pinched my cheeks. I smiled and tried to look as though I was not dying, and they let me on that plane.

Once I arrived back at the hospital, they checked me into Emergency and put me straight on an IV. The doctors told me that I could not leave again because of how sick I was. It was really hard to be so ill. I had a Russian doctor who had never heard the Gospel. He actually had never seen a Bible, which shocked me. He asked me about my book with the "gold pages" that I kept underlining. Then he told me that my time was coming to an end and that I should prepare for the inevitable. He even told me I should write my epitaph. That was not too nice to hear.

Rolland was with me, praying day and night in the hospital. One day he asked me if I needed anything. I had forgotten my running shoes in Mozambique, and I wanted a new pair. He did not even question me. We had been married for over 25 years at that time, so he just said okay and went out to a few malls until he found the right shoes. Instead of flowers or slippers, he came back with running shoes and put them by my bed. Each day, I looked at those shoes and believed I would run again soon.

I continued to press in to the presence of God, even though I was in the most intense pain of my life. I was extremely weak, and the antibiotics made me worse. Even when I was in this state, people were drawn to my room. Several got healed, and others got saved. Nurses lined up until after 2:00 a.m. because they wanted prayer. The presence of God was so strong that even the workers changing my sheets started to weep when they entered. It was a powerful and awesome time of seeing God's presence manifested in a dark place.

During this time, I could barely even read the Bible. I mostly listened to it on audio. When I was strong enough to read a little,

I was drawn to the book of Zechariah. I read it over and over, and the Lord spoke to me through it in a powerful way. I also listened to Bill Johnson's healing series several times. Rolland continued to pray for me each day. I felt as if I were pushing on a rock, believing one day it would move. I never stopped worshiping Jesus. I actually felt happy because the presence of God was so strong. At the same time, I was bizarrely weak.

From Bad to Worse

In the midst of my struggle for life, a contractor from another nation, who was working for us in Mozambique, told Rolland that he had finished building our mission school. Rolland was so distraught by my condition that he told the team to pay the bill without verifying the contractor's report. The contractor then fled the country and ran off with somewhere around $160,000, even though he had never finished the work. That was all the money our ministry had.

This was such a dark time. I was dying, and we had been robbed of a huge sum of money. Those at our mission base were also dealing with malaria, dysentery and problems with the government. For someone to steal that much money on top of everything else was extremely rough. It was one of the hardest times of my life.

Even though God's presence was so strong in my little hospital room, I could not believe it could be that hard. I felt discouraged.

Then I heard God say, *What did I say to you?*

I remembered Randy Clark's prophecy over me in Toronto years before, when he said, "Now, Heidi, the Lord wants to know, do you want the nation of Mozambique?"

I knew we did not have the nation yet. We were in the north and everything God had done up to that point had been awesome, but I would not call it the transformation of a nation—just the bare beginnings. I was willing to die if that was what God wanted. Because of unfulfilled prophecies, though, it did not feel as if it was my time to go.

During my stay in that hospital room, a dove would come every morning and fly around my window, look at me and then fly off. The dove would then come back in the cool of the evening and sleep right next to my window.

Seeing that dove, I felt that the Holy Spirit was saying to me, *I am looking for a dwelling place. I want a place where I can rest. The Body of Christ is being eaten away by flesh-eating diseases, and they don't even know it. I want to heal them and rest in them. When My glory rests on them, no sickness can live and nothing can eat away at their flesh; nothing will be able to take them out.*

I was so encouraged by this little white dove God had sent just for me. But I was still in a fight. I continued to press in to His glorious presence. I called out to have more.

He commissioned me by saying, *Tell the Church that I want to live, rest and abide in them. I don't just want to visit them; I want to take over their whole body. I want all of who they are. I want everything.*

I already had canceled my commitments in Mozambique and around the world because I was getting even sicker. My open wounds were not closing, and the doctor said there was nothing left anyone could do for me but try one last medication called "Compassion" antibiotic.

I thought it was amazingly prophetic that the last straw was called "Compassion." In the Bible, after the sick had tried everything else, Jesus came in and healed them with compassion.

On day 32 of my being sick with no improvement, they took me in a medical vehicle to a top specialist to see what would happen next.

The South African specialist, a Christian, looked at me with tears running down his face and said, "I've heard about what you do and how you rescue children and reach the lost. I'm so sorry because there is nothing I can do for you. You just need to prepare for the end." He also told me, "You do not owe me any money, because I am unable to help you."

When I heard him say these things, it was the first time I got really excited. This was a perfect chance for God to do something really big. There was no hope, no medical solution, and our ministry was completely broke. Two of the doctors had told me I was going to die. I do not think it could have been stacked up any higher against us or have gotten any harder. We also had other stressful things happening to our family and in other relationships. This was probably one of the lowest times of my life. It felt as if everything were crashing down. It would have been easier to just forget it all, give up and die. It was that hard.

When I returned to the other hospital, Rolland and I prayed and asked God what He wanted us to do. We were not sure if we were supposed to prepare people for my death and plan my funeral or what. I had been invited to Toronto, but no one expected me to go because I had canceled everything except that invitation.

During this time of sickness, I had already tried to step into my healing by first checking myself out of the hospital in Malaysia and then later in South Africa. Both times when I stepped out by faith, my healing still did not come. In fact, I got worse. Going to Toronto would be the third time of trying to walk by faith and not by sight into my healing. I like sharing about my failures because sometimes people try things and fail, and then they do not try again. I failed the first time I checked myself out of the hospital. I just got sicker. I tried it again and got even sicker. Toronto would be my last try, because I was literally on the verge of death.

When I told people I wanted to check myself out of the hospital once again, everyone told me I was crazy. I said I wanted to see the top specialist in Canada. The nurses all chuckled because they knew I was going to meet with the Great Physician. Obviously, I could meet with Jesus in my room, and I had done that. But for whatever reason, He did not want to heal me there. Instead, He healed everyone else who came in.

Off to Toronto for More, Lord!

I said to Rolland, "Let's go to Toronto. I think I'm supposed to go there and preach."

I had been healed there in the past, so I knew there could be a special grace there. Rolland immediately supported this decision. I called John and Carol Arnott, and they said it was okay for me to come, but they encouraged me to soak rather than preach. They also said they would have an IV set up in the hospitality room for me once I arrived.

My flight to Toronto was the worst and most painful flight of my entire life. I had a raging fever and open, running sores. They would never have let me on the plane if they had known I was dying. Again, I put blush on my cheeks to add some color to my pale face, and I smiled as I walked on the plane.

When I arrived in Toronto and got to the hotel, my health deteriorated even more. I was super-thin, and my skin was whitish green. I thought this might be the end, but at the same time, I was thankful that I had at least made it to Toronto.

When it was time to go to the service, my friend Betty, a security guard at the church, had a pillow and blanket ready for me. As I lay there, people thought I was soaking in God's presence. While that was partially true, I also was struggling to stay alive. They encouraged me to go back into the hospitality room to rest, but I did not want to leave the place of worship.

As I was lying there, everything was spinning. I was crazy sick and in pain, weaker than weak. I remember thinking that if I fell down, no one would notice because they would just think I was slain in the Spirit.

Carol told me that I did not have to preach because of the state I was in. But I knew I was called to preach that day. When the time came, with all the strength I could muster, I walked onto that stage. I do not think I have ever been that sick or that weak in my entire life. I literally held on to the pulpit for dear life so I would not fall over.

I began to preach about what God had shown me from Zechariah in the hospital room, about becoming a resting place for God. As soon as I got to the part in Zechariah 2:5 where the Lord says He will be *a wall of fire around about you and the glory within you*, the glory of God hit me powerfully. It went from my head to my toes three times like electricity. That was the precise moment when God's love broke in during one of the darkest times of my life.

After this surge of energy, all weakness left. I was completely and utterly healed. Strength continued to increase as I preached. After I was done preaching, the Lord told me to dance. So right there on that stage, I danced in His glorious and life-giving love, giving an offering of thanksgiving to the One I love.

When I got back to the hotel, every open wound that had existed for 33 days had completely closed. For 33 days, I had been in one of the biggest fights of my life. The fight was finally over, and I was healed. I will never forget that day as long as I live.

When I woke up the next morning super-early because of jet lag, I heard the Lord tell me to put on the running shoes that Rolland had bought me and run. I ran for one hour straight with no fatigue. I ran as if I were in the best shape of my life. I was completely and totally healed.

I felt the Lord say, *Tell the Church it's time to run, move, go and reach the lost.*

I felt that He wanted to heal the Body of Christ of flesh-eating diseases and teach them how to let His glory abide. He also spoke to me more deeply about how He longed to be a resting place.

Normally, I never watch or listen to myself preach, but this time I wanted to see with my own eyes what God had done in that moment, because it was so powerful. I want to share with you that exact moment when God's healing power broke in during one of the hardest times of my life. I believe that this will release fresh hope in you as you endure until the end. You can watch the actual sermon on Catch the Fire TV on YouTube, at "Session D (Soaking in God's Glory 2005) Heidi Baker." (This can be accessed at https://www.youtube.com/watch?v=2zXpPt-NEsQ. My sermon starts at 2:24:00.)

God is worthy even of our suffering. When you face suffering, go through hard times or are in the midst of a storm, I encourage you to pray in the Holy Spirit, including the gift of tongues (see 1 Corinthians 14:14–15; Jude 20–21). Spend time worshiping and fixing your eyes on Jesus. Ask the Holy Spirit to rest in you and possess you. If you are experiencing pain or encountering hardships, ask for more possession of the Holy Spirit so that you will find joy in the midst of the suffering. Ask that you will be so full of Him that no matter what happens, even if you die, you are content, knowing that you will go straight to Jesus.

When God's Love Broke Through

I now close with some excerpts from the actual sermon I gave that unforgettable night, October 20, 2005, in Toronto, when God's love broke in during my darkest hour. These are the highlights. May what was released during my moment of breakthrough release hope, strength, joy and courage in you as you contend to be a holy habitation. May you become a resting place for the living God, no matter what storms may come your way.

> God, I pray that You would find a resting place in each one. I pray that destinies would be fulfilled. I pray that there would not be one abortion, not one aborted ministry and not one aborted call. Fulfill Your destiny in each one of us, Jesus.
>
> I heard the Lord say that Satan is trying to steal people's destinies. He is trying to cause exhaustion to creep into the renewal. This is insidious, and we are to fight. The way we fight is by becoming a resting place for Him and by being fully possessed by the Holy Spirit. There is a method, but it is not the method of man. There is a way that we will become victorious, but it is a way that is so completely opposite of the way that we think.
>
> God is saying, *Lie down, and let Me love you. This is the way you are going to fight.*
>
> I have been contending for full possession. When bacteria came in and tried to destroy me and take my very life, I understood the fight. There was a fight going on between the flesh and the spirit that was literally trying to take my life. There is an enemy who would take the very life and suck it out of the Church. However, the method of our warfare is entirely different than we thought. Our life is not our own. We are to be a people fully possessed by the Holy Spirit. We are to be the ones who carry the glory of the Lord wherever we are.
>
> I urge you to fight to become a resting place and a holy habitation for the One who is altogether beautiful. When anything tries to come and steal from you, just say, "No! I am contending for one thing—to be a holy habitation for the glory of the Lord. I want to be a carrier of God's presence to the ends of the earth. I want to love Him without limit. I want to lay down my life for love and become a holy habitation."

The way I fight is not by running harder; it is by lying down and letting the Holy Spirit take all of me.

Zechariah 2:5 [NASB] says, "'For I,' declares the LORD, 'will be a wall of fire around her, and I will be the glory in her midst.'"

Who is the glory in our midst? The King, glorious and mighty. He is the King who is always in our midst, no matter what comes against us! He is a wall of fire that surrounds us. We have to say no to everything that tries to come in and destroy us, everything that would keep us from fixing our eyes on the One who is altogether beautiful. We have to say no to every bit of darkness and say yes to every bit of light. He is the King.

Will you fulfill your destiny? Your destiny is to become a dwelling place for the Most High God. Wherever that destiny takes you, you are to be a dwelling place for Him so that He lives and breathes in you, so that [even though this is ungrammatical] you are that laid-down servant, so that you say, "God, I don't care what it takes or what it costs. I am just going to lie down and be a servant. I am going to give You all that I am—every breath, every heartbeat and every thought. I am going to give it to You, Jesus, because You are all that matters to me."

Then, if you are in a hospital or a university or the bush or the garbage dump or wherever it is that you reside, you are a dwelling place for the Holy Spirit. When this happens, the only thing that can take place around you will be miracles, life and beauty.

The Lord is asking us to complete the task and finish the race. It is not a sprint. It is a marathon. We need to drink of Him as we run. I want to encourage you to run into the fire and stay there. Stay red-hot and full of fire until the end. As we carry the glory of the Most High God, as we fight the fight, knowing that Jesus is always victorious, will we be the laid-down servant lovers? Will we walk in humility? Will we rise up or lie down? Everything about the fight looks different, beloved of God. As we lie down and let Him love us, as we soak and as we live in the glory, He fills us with His power. Our mind is transformed, and we become the very light of Jesus in a dark world. And we are unstoppable.

But there is a fight. He is our wall of fire. We experience the fire of the Lord because He is the fire! He burns away everything that does not belong, but He also puts a hedge around us and says, "Live inside the fire. Don't run away from the fire; run into the fire. And let it burn—let it blaze. 'I will be a wall of fire around her, and I will be the glory in her midst.'"

The Lord of glory is in our midst. He is inside us and inside the Church corporately. Oh, beloved of God, you are called to carry the glory!

We are not called just to sing about the glory and get together and worship. We are called to carry it into the darkness and to live a life of fight by lying down and by giving our lives for the One who is beautiful. "'Not by might nor by power, but by my Spirit,' says the LORD" [Zechariah 4:6 NASB]. The wave of His Spirit will grow and grow, and we will see the most incredible end-time harvest come in. Darkness will become light like the bright noon sun.

Will you fulfill your destiny? Will you be a fearless lover, running into the darkness by giving your life? Will you lie down and let God love you and pour so much of His presence into you that even if you are in a hospital room, streams of people come in because they can feel the very presence of God? Will you become a holy habitation, a resting place? More will happen in one day in His presence than in a previous lifetime. Contend for full possession. Ask God to pour His presence through you. Know that by lying down, you stand up, and that by becoming nothing, you become His.

The Lord wants to fully possess you and become one with you. He wants to pulsate and breathe His life in and through you. He wants to pick you up on the wings of His Spirit and soar with you throughout the earth.

May you run and not grow weary, walk and not faint. May you mount up with wings like eagles and soar. May you continually fight by lying down. May you cling to Jesus always, no matter what the cost.

Compelled by His love,
Heidi Baker

Heidi and Rolland Baker will go anywhere and do anything for Jesus. They began Iris Global (previously Iris Ministries) in 1980 and now have ministry bases around the world, with the largest focus in Mozambique. Information about their ministry is available at https://www.irisglobal.org.

4

When Love Breaks Through

By Mahesh Chavda

Greater love has no one than this, that one lay down
his life for his friends.

John 15:13 NASB

More than thirty years ago, I went into the innermost
parts of Africa to proclaim the Good News of Jesus
Christ. I will never forget flying over the open field
where we would be ministering and seeing thousands of people
coming through the jungle from all directions to meet us.

Our hosts told me, "They have come to meet you. Many of
them have walked for seven days to hear the Word of God."

We often think it is a hardship for us in the Western world
to drive a few hours to a meeting. These people were so hungry
for God that they walked for many days to hear the Gospel. I

realized that this might be their first and only time hearing the Good News of Jesus.

I asked the Lord, "What should I share with these people who may never hear Your Word again?"

He said, "Tell them about Jesus."

That first night, I gave the simple message of the Gospel of salvation. Mid-message, I heard a roar ripple through the crowd. People were clapping and shouting wildly. A young man, sixteen years old, emerged from the commotion and began running. The villagers recognized him instantly. I later learned he had been born a cripple. His whole life, he had dragged his body around in a little makeshift wheelbarrow. When I proclaimed Jesus, the glory and creative power of God came and straightened out his legs and back. He jumped up and was soon running around the crowd. Faith had come, and when faith comes, miracles happen. I have seen this time and time again through my international ministry. When faith comes, miracles happen.

The boy's mother fell in the dirt and came crawling toward me, throwing dust onto her head. It was the traditional way her tribe would approach a chief.

"Thank you, great chief, for coming from America and healing my son," she said.

I picked her up out of the dirt and told her, "I am no great king. I am the lowest of the servants of the greatest King. His name is Jesus. He healed your son."

That miracle was the first of hundreds of extraordinary miracles. The atmosphere was pregnant with glory, and the power of God was present to heal. News spread, and the crowds grew. Night after night and miracle after miracle, the blind saw, the lame walked, cancers fell away, the oppressed were set free and the poorest of the poor received the greatest miracle of all, Jesus Christ as Lord and Savior.

A Knock at the Door

Late one night after one of these meetings, I heard a knock at my door. Standing there was one of the local pastors.

"We've just received word of a little child in one of the villages who is dying from cerebral malaria," he said. "The mother has heard about your healing services. She is asking if you will come and pray for her son."

As we walked through the night, the pastor began unfolding the young woman's story for me. This single mother of five-year-old twin boys was struggling to support her family and grow as a Christian. Five years earlier, she had been a happy bride and had given birth to her twin sons. In her tribal tradition at that time, however, twins were feared as a bad omen. Her husband divorced her, her family disowned her and she was forced to leave the village.

With no other means of support for her children, this mother had resorted to selling her body to buy food. It was in this desperate situation that the Good News of the Gospel of the Kingdom had come to her through this local pastor. She had put her trust in Jesus and had consequently given up prostitution, turning solely to God to provide for her family.

We reached the mud hut where the woman lived. A tattered cloth hung over the entrance. I stooped to enter, and there, in the dim glow of a single candle, sat the mother on the dirt floor, rocking her young son in her arms. Nearby, another boy lay sleeping on a pallet. With pleading eyes full of hope, the woman gently lifted her precious child to me.

My heart sank. It was evident that the child I took into my arms had already been dead for some hours. His little body was cold and was already beginning to stiffen. I sat down next to the mother, and for more than an hour I prayed, asking the Lord to restore him back to this precious, faith-filled mother. After some time, I understood that God was not going to raise the little boy on that day.

I will never forget the crushing sadness I felt as I handed the dead boy back to his mother. With tears streaming from her eyes, she looked up to heaven and spoke softly in her native tongue.

"Take him gently with both hands, Jesus," this mother prayed. Echoing the words of King David at the loss of his son thousands of years before, she continued in her tender voice, "Now he will no longer run to me, but I will run to him."

I stood outside that hut for a long time, feeling tired and alone. I could not help feeling as though I had failed this poor mother. As my heart ached for her, a wind swirled around me. I sensed the presence of the Holy Spirit.

Out of that wind, I heard a Voice: "Mahesh, as you have been faithful, you will see great things."

This is part of God's encouragement for you in your darkest hour: It is God's nature to love, heal and deliver His children. He is the God of miracles. But He is also sovereign. He is God. Glory, and therefore the real works and miracles, come from Him. Not seeing a miracle at the moment when my heart went out to this young mother was hard. But my wife, Bonnie, and I have learned over the years that we do not ask why. We know that in all things God does not change, and in everything, His love and compassion in the midst of our loss, disappointment or hope deferred will bring Him glory. How we respond in those moments creates a platform for God to move in our lives and show forth His mighty works.

The Unexpected Event

A few months after I returned home from that trip, I received a letter from a group of pastors in Zaire—the Belgian Congo. The letter was typed on a crumpled piece of yellow paper. It was full of mistakes, and clearly some of the typewriter keys were damaged. Yet when I read the humble plea of the pastors, I sensed the voice of the Lord.

They wrote to me, "We believe that if you will come, the destiny and future of our nation will be changed."

On the surface, it seemed improbable that the authors of this crude invitation would be able to host the outreach they described. "We expect hundreds of thousands in attendance and many, many lives will be changed," they wrote.

Bonnie and I sensed the unction of the Holy Spirit in this invitation, so we did not immediately decline. I had already made plans to return to Zambia with Derek Prince the following year. I decided to look into what it would cost to add a flight to Zaire to my itinerary. The total cost of the extra flight was 27 dollars! It was the confirmation I needed. I accepted the invitation.

Then our story took an unexpected turn. In February, we found out we were expecting our fourth child. Bonnie immediately began experiencing complications. She was diagnosed with placenta previa centralis, a dangerous condition that puts mother and baby at risk of death. After a number of tests, the doctors essentially told us to abort our baby. They could not find a heartbeat or any other sign of life in her womb, and Bonnie's life was in danger. The physician in charge assured us that if Bonnie continued the pregnancy and the baby was alive, our child would only live for a few days. If it did live longer, it would be in a vegetative state.

As if to confirm his words, Bonnie began to hemorrhage. Things were not looking good. But when we asked God what to do, we heard only silence. So we waited.

We learned something in that time. Bonnie and I were going along on the mission of God. We were hearing the Lord, obeying Him, following Him and seeing tremendous miracles wherever we would go. Now we faced this unexpected event. It felt as though God had left and gone to Kansas! I wanted to ask, "God! Did I miss You somewhere? Did I do something wrong? Where are You?" But we learned that sometimes, when God seems the most silent, He is preparing to do His greatest miracles.

Now in addition to my pastoral roles and travel itinerary, I assumed the role of Mr. Mom to our three children under the age of six. Bonnie was put on complete bed rest. As she lay in bed day after day, her eyes rested on one of the gifts I had brought home from my latest trip to Africa, a small handmade painting of an African man making his way through a dense green jungle.

Bonnie began to rehearse the miracles from that trip—the thousands of people who had come to know Jesus, the incredible healings of lifelong blindness, paralysis and devastating disease. She recalled the faces of the desperate families who struggled without even the most primitive medical care. She made that man in the picture a point of contact for her prayers. If the devil was going to attack us and the life of our unborn child, she was determined that she was going to make him sorry. She began praying into my upcoming trip, asking the Lord to do something great for all those who had no other helper.

I was praying with all my might, too. I used every spiritual weapon and discipline I knew of, asking the Lord for a breakthrough.

Finally, one afternoon God spoke: "I will give you a secret weapon."

I got out my notebook and Bible, expecting the Lord to download a Scripture to pray, or something I could do that would add fuel to my prayers. Instead, I heard the most unusual thing.

God said, "You and Bonnie need to laugh your way through this. This is your key to victory."

I wanted to remind God that there was not a single part of our situation that was even remotely funny. But I also knew to obey. So I went out and got some tapes from our favorite comedian to help prime the pump for us to laugh. From that day, for an hour or so each afternoon Bonnie and I would lie on our bed and listen to hilarious stories and laugh and laugh. We soon found we had more faith, more hope, more love and more peace, even though our circumstances continued to worsen.

Twenty-one weeks into the pregnancy, there were still no signs of life in Bonnie's womb. We continued to wait for God to speak. He seemed to be hiding His face regarding our baby.

Then one day, Bonnie heard the Lord in that voice that sounds like your own, but that says things you know are not your own thoughts: "Bonnie, you will have a son. Name him Aaron, because I am going to make the rod of his life bud like Aaron's rod of old."

The Lord gave her Numbers 17 (NKJV) to hold on to:

And you shall write Aaron's name on the rod of Levi. . . . Then you shall place them in the tabernacle of meeting before the Testimony, where I meet with you. . . . And Moses placed the rods before the LORD in the tabernacle of witness.

Now it came to pass on the next day that Moses went into the tabernacle of witness, and behold, the rod of Aaron, of the house of Levi, had sprouted and put forth buds, had produced blossoms and yielded ripe almonds.

The next week, Bonnie got a phone call from a friend in Texas whom she had not spoken with in several years.

"I was in my prayer closet," this friend said. "I have never gotten a word like this in my life, but I believe God spoke to me. He said you are going to have a son. You are supposed to name him Aaron."

With this amazing confirmation, we stood firmly on what God had promised. We needed it!

Darkness Came before the Light

Things went from bad to worse. Bonnie's water broke, and then her placenta died and fell out. Bonnie died twice as she hemorrhaged. Then, in her twenty-fifth week, Bonnie's doctor felt that we had come to the point where he had to do an emergency C-section to save her life.

Bonnie was rushed into surgery. The operating room was filled with medical personnel. Just as the anesthesiologist was about to administer the anesthesia, Bonnie says another Man entered the room. He walked through the closed doors and walked to the head of the table where she lay. As His belly came in contact with her head, rays of light and love and power flowed out of Him and into her body. As they passed through her, she says she saw her hand lift up, and she heard herself announce to the doctor, "I can have this baby naturally."

Everything stopped. Another Authority had spoken, and every medical person in the room bowed to that will. Within a few minutes, that Voice surrounded Bonnie's womb. She soon heard five tiny little mews like a newborn kitten.

She looked at the doctor. He looked terrified by what he held in his hands.

Bonnie said, "It's a boy, isn't it?"

The doctor nodded his head.

She said, "His name is Aaron. He will live and not die."

That was the beginning of our journey. Aaron weighed less than one pound at birth. He had a staph infection, blood in his spinal fluid indicating a brain hemorrhage, and lungs that were not fully developed. His ears were still just flaps of skin. His tiny face was smashed flat from the lack of amniotic fluid to cushion it. His dry skin was bruised everywhere.

That was not even the worst of it. A portion of Aaron's intestines had died and calcified, and his tiny body was filled with gangrene. He was so small that Bonnie's wedding ring could fit onto his thigh. His fingertips were so small that his nails were invisible. This was the son of whom God had said He would "make his rod bud."

The Radical Call to Obey

In the midst of this crisis, I was scheduled to return to Africa on a promise I had made the previous year, that year when I had sat in that little hut with the young mother whose five-year-old son had died of cerebral malaria. I agonized over what to do. I recalled the simple plea the Zairian pastors had written on that crumpled sheet of paper. I felt the Lord had clearly called me to go. I did not want to disappoint the people who would be waiting for me.

But I also did not want to leave Bonnie at such a vulnerable time. It seemed clear that unless the Lord intervened in a most dramatic fashion, Aaron had only a few more days to live. I knew that if I went, I would never see my son alive on this side of glory again. Worse yet, Bonnie would have to bury him alone.

I started making plans to cancel the trip. When Bonnie realized what I was doing, she insisted that I go.

She told me, "Your presence here cannot make Aaron live or die. But you carry miracles. Your presence out there may mean some other woman's son will live."

I will never forget the day I kissed Aaron good-bye, thinking it would be the last time I would see my baby boy in this world. With my heart breaking, I headed to Africa to proclaim the Good News to the poor in obedience to the call God had placed on our lives.

The only correspondence I had had with my hosts in Zaire was that I would accept their invitation and would arrive in Kinshasa on Sunday, June 9. I never heard another word from my hosts. I could only hope that the man who invited me would be at the airport to meet me.

He was there. As we drove toward town, I inquired about plans for the campaign.

"Have you scheduled a seminar for the mornings?" I asked.

"Yes, sir," he replied.

"And have you made arrangements for open meetings in the evenings?"

"Yes, sir."

"About how many should we expect at the open meetings?" I asked. I was hoping there might be as many as five hundred.

"About fifty thousand, sir."

"Fifty thousand!"

"Yes, sir," he said, seeming almost apologetic. "That is because it is during the week. We will be able to have a big crowd on the weekend."

About two thousand attended the first seminar on Monday morning. As I finished speaking, I heard the Holy Spirit tell me that there was a woman in the crowd who was dying of cancer, and that I should invite her to come forward. In response, an elderly woman, her body covered with cancerous tumors, came walking through the crowd. As she neared the stage, the power of the Holy Spirit came upon her and knocked her to the ground, as if by a physical blow. By the time I reached her, the tumors had disappeared. She rose to her feet and went away dancing for joy. The Lord had healed her.

News of this miraculous healing spread like wildfire. That night, instead of the fifty thousand my hosts had expected, almost one hundred thousand people showed up. There were paralytics, lepers and people with AIDS. I had never seen anything like it. Some of the sick people were brought to the meeting in wheelbarrows, soaking in their own urine and excrement.

Many who were lame were healed that night, including a number of little children. It is difficult to describe the overwhelming emotion I felt as I saw those little ones walk without canes or crutches for the first time in years, perhaps for the first time in their lives. The manifestation of the power of God was so strong that witch doctors and sorcerers were repenting and accepting Jesus Christ as their Savior and Lord. For them to take this radical step in public was a spiritual earthquake.

Then the Voice of God Came

The crowds continued to grow. By Wednesday morning, there were fifty thousand people crowded into Kasavubu Square for the morning meeting. I had just finished my message and stepped back from the microphone when all of a sudden, the same wind that had surrounded me outside that young mother's hut surrounded me again. Despite the throngs of people milling about, it felt to me as though the world had simply fallen silent, and time itself had stopped.

Then the same quiet, gentle, loving voice of the Holy Spirit said, "Mahesh, there is a man here whose son died this morning. Call him up, because today I am going to do a great thing."

I stepped back to the microphone and said, "There is a man here whose son died this morning. Where is that man?"

The crowd was buzzing, waiting to see what would happen next. Those who had been present at our earlier meetings had already seen several amazing healings and miracles performed in the name of the Lord Jesus. It electrified the atmosphere as people sensed that the Holy Spirit had something special planned for this moment.

A few seconds passed, and then a man came running toward the platform. He threaded his way through the crowd, waving his hand in the air and crying, "It is I! It is I!"

As he came toward me, I studied him. He was tall and built like a boxer. I could see in his eyes a mixture of hope and fear, faith and doubt. I asked him no questions, not even his name. I simply placed my hands on his head and prayed a simple prayer.

"Lord, the same Spirit that raised Your Son from the dead go now and quicken the body of this man's son!"

When I finished, the man gazed at me for a moment, then nodded his head one time as if to say thank you, and then he ran off again. The crowd parted to let him pass.

By that evening's service, we had begun to hear amazing reports about the tall man who had come forward for prayer. His name was Mulamba Manikai. His six-year-old son, Katshinyi, whose name means, "don't be afraid of Satan," had died early that morning of cerebral malaria. It was the same sickness that had taken the twin son of the poor mother I had prayed with the year before.

Katshinyi had been pronounced dead by doctors at Kinshasa's Mikondo Clinic. His body was taken to the Mama Yemo Hospital morgue to await burial. His unbelieving uncle, Quamba, held Katshinyi's dead body while his father ran to get the paperwork needed to bury his son.

On his way across town to get the required forms, Mulamba heard the Lord say, *My servant is in Kinshasa. Go to him.*

He detoured to the square where I was speaking, arriving just as I ended my message. His heart dropped when he saw that there were fifty thousand people between him and the platform, and there was no way he could make his way through the crowd before I left. But then, as he gave up hope of reaching me, I stepped back to the microphone and delivered the word calling him forward.

At noon on June 12, 1985, as I prayed for the dead boy's father in front of fifty thousand people in Kasavubu Square, Katshinyi suddenly sneezed twice and sat up in his uncle's arms.

The boy looked around and asked, "Where is my father?" Then he turned to his mother and said, "I am hungry. Give me something to eat."

Here is a word of note for you: If you want to be in the resurrection business, always be sure to take a sandwich. They come back hungry!

As I recalled Mulamba threading his way toward me through the crowd, I remembered the night a year before, when I had stood in the darkness outside that little mud hut and the Voice had spoken to me out of the wind, "As you are faithful, you will see great things."

Six-year-old Katshinyi had died from the same dreaded cerebral malaria that had taken the life of that young mother's precious five-year-old son. One year later, I saw the resurrection power of Jesus raise this other mother's son from the dead. And there was yet more glory, and more mercy and more miracles to come home to us.

What You Sow, You Will Reap

While I was away sacrificially obeying the call of God on my life, God did what only God can do. Step by step, trial by trial, our son Aaron lived. Day after day he gained life, health and strength. Today Aaron is an athletic, handsome, intelligent young man who loves and serves God.

"The secret things belong to the LORD our God, but those things which are revealed belong to us and to our children forever" (Deuteronomy 29:29 NKJV).

Jesus is the same yesterday, today and forever. He reveals Himself as Jehovah Rapha, the Lord who heals. He reveals Himself as the great God of miracles.

He is the God who is pure love, and His love always breaks through. What you sow, you will reap. When you will sow seeds of kindness into someone else's darkness, God's love will break through for you in your darkest moment.

Living in the glory,
Mahesh Chavda

Mahesh and Bonnie Chavda lead Chavda Ministries International, a worldwide apostolic ministry; pastor All Nations Church in Charlotte, North Carolina; and spearhead The Watch of the Lord, a global prayer movement. Information about their ministries is available at http://www.chavdaministries.org.

5

Wrapped in Love

By Barbara J. Yoder

> Praise be to . . . the God of all comfort, who com-
> forts us in all our troubles, so that we can comfort
> those in any trouble with the comfort we ourselves
> receive from God.
>
> 2 Corinthians 1:3–4 NIV

I thought I was a fairly good planner, as well as an accurate assessor of most situations. My husband, Paul, was not doing well because of a chronic, potentially fatal physical condition. I believed everything would work out, though, and he would be fine.

It was the third week of January, and I had just finished cooking supper. As soon as we sat down to enjoy it together, I looked at Paul and immediately heard these words: *Your husband is not going to make it.*

Having had many years of experience listening to the voice of God, I knew this was not fear, the devil or my imagination. God was alerting me that time was short.

Paul had struggled with his condition for a year, and it had taken a turn for the worse. He sensed it, and I could feel him slowly letting go of life as we know it. He was weary with the process of fighting for his life. But I had never visited this place of losing. I was sure he would beat it, and God would heal him. I am just a positive person by nature, so the words I heard shocked my inner world.

The Agonizing Pain

How do I find words to express the emotions that suddenly erupted within? I could feel this loud, piercing wail taking form within me. The feelings were so deep, so raw and so eruptive that I was on the verge of a sudden explosive outburst. I flew out of my chair and dashed to the bathroom. As I ran from the table (which was totally out of character for me), I told my husband I had just had an especially strong hot flash and needed a cold shower. I had never had a hot flash in my life, but I did not know what else to tell him. I did not want to tell him what I had just heard.

I will never forget standing in that shower sobbing, using the running water to keep him from hearing me. Thirty minutes later, I emerged to eat my supper. Somehow I maintained a semblance of sanity. I could not and would not tell him what I had heard. I did not want to diminish his faith, send him into a depression or create hopelessness. For all he knew, I had simply had an out-of-control hot flash.

The next day, I called Bill Hamon of Christian International in Florida. I wanted to make sure I was not hearing amiss. But more than anything, I did not want to believe what I had heard.

I wanted someone to tell me it was not what I thought it was, that Paul was going to die.

Bishop Hamon kindly responded by making a commitment to fast and pray with me about the situation. But I did not receive another response from him until almost a month later, after Paul died.

The weekend after I heard those disturbing words at the supper table, I had to speak in Windsor, Ontario. I will never forget Paul driving me there on Saturday afternoon.

When we arrived at the hotel, Paul said, "Can I stay with you?"

That was so unlike him. He was always responsible for home base when I was called to speak elsewhere. I knew that he was sensing something, and he did not want to be alone. Nevertheless, he had to get back to lead the Sunday morning church service at home. Though I was the senior pastor, he covered for me when I was away. Both of us agreed that he needed to return home. It broke my heart to let him go, knowing what was before us and realizing that he did not know what I knew—that the end was near.

Identifying with Jesus

I wept most of the night alone in that hotel room. I wept for my husband, wept for myself, wept for knowing that losing him was sitting on me like a piece of gum stuck to the bottom of a chair. I wondered how in the world I was going to minister that Sunday, given the intensity of feelings I was experiencing. By faith I had to move forward, believing that God would be my strength in the midst of my overwhelming weakness. We are so fragile at times, yet we really do have this treasure in earthen vessels (see 2 Corinthians 4:7).

I could not pray, not really pray—not as I so often did when crises loomed before me. I could only silently feel this desperate cry to God from the depths of me, knowing what was about to take place. I tried to read the psalms, but all I could feel was pain. I felt I was experiencing some of what Jesus must have felt in the Garden of Gethsemane, when He begged God to let this cup pass from Him. The cup would not leave me. It was fastened to my hand. I knew I was entering into a deeper identification with Jesus through it.

For the first time, I had a real sense of what it must have felt like for Jesus to agonize over His future in the Garden alone. Although it was not my life being taken, in a sense it was. Because my life as I knew it was about to change. The man I loved and was joined to was just about to leave me for good. At that time, it was no consolation to think that he would be with Jesus. My pain was that he would no longer be with me. In that pain, I began to realize what it was to be one in marriage. It was more than theory; it was also a feeling of oneness such that if one partner left, the other lost part of himself or herself.

After returning home from speaking in Ontario, I stumbled through the next few days and found myself returning to my analytical ways. I thought if Paul was not going to live, then his death probably would occur in June. I had six weeks around that time when I was going to be home, not traveling, and God was practical. In my mind, He was alerting me so that I could plan. Never in my wildest imagination did I think that it would take place in a couple of weeks.

Then the Morning Came

Two or three weeks after I heard that word from the Lord, I took Chuck Pierce, another trusted prophetic friend, to Detroit on February 8 to speak. I turned off my cell phone so that it did not ring during the service. When Paul returned home that day, he left me a written message that he had gone downstairs to sleep because he did not feel well. He did not want me to awaken him when I arrived home.

For some reason, nothing computed. When I read his note, I did not put two and two together. I should have checked on him. The doctor had told us that if Paul either started bleeding or developed a fever, we should get him to the emergency room immediately. I did not link his feeling unwell with either a fever or bleeding, so off to bed I went.

On awakening, I noticed Paul's coat was still on the dining room chair. *Strange!* I thought. *He was supposed to go to the hospital to get a blood transfusion this morning.*

It was 8:30, and he always left around 7:30. I rushed downstairs to wake him up for his appointment. There was no waking him up. He was gone. Sometime during the night, he had died.

Immediately I called 911. When the police arrived, they noted that he had been dead for a while. I did not want to touch him, feel him or try to resuscitate him. I just wanted to get out of the room. It was too shocking for me. I did not even think about trying to raise him from the dead. He was gone. I was in a total state of shock.

The Power of Worship

Right away I called Paul's children to let them know. Once they arrived and I told them the story, something inside me said, *It's time to worship!* Years before, when I first fell in love with Jesus, I learned the power of worship through lifting up my voice and praising God for all He is, all He has done for me and who He is to me. We worship what or who we are in love with, and I had a revelation of worship. Worship became a lifestyle as well as an action for me. I knew the power of worship.

If I chose to worship in this moment rather than become hysterical, I would set my course for the future. I knew I had to make a decision to set my course. There was no option for me. I asked the children to come into the bedroom with me, and I closed the door. The police were in the living room, and we needed privacy.

I began to worship, lifting up my voice and lovingly pouring out praise to God. I thanked Him for all the years I had had with Paul, for God's goodness to me through Paul, for the love we had shared and the many experiences that together had transformed us. And then I began to worship God for who He is.

Worship poured out of me as I lifted up my voice. Paul was still lying dead in the house. His body could not be removed until a full investigation of his death was complete. In spite of that, I was suddenly lifted into another sphere. It was as if time stood still and I was in the presence of God. I was in a realm where I understood how the songwriter Horatio Spafford wrote the hymn "It Is Well with My Soul." All four of his daughters had drowned after a collision at sea. But like Spafford, I had found that place where I was cocooned in God for that moment. It was in His love. But this was only the first thread in the tapestry that would wrap me with God's love in the midst of loss.

The Waiting Room

How do I describe the time between my husband's death and the final moment of recognizing that my life as I knew it was over? I call that time "the waiting room." It was that interim week when calls poured in, visitors came, funeral arrangements were made, the obituary was written and burial plots were bought. Then the end came—the funeral and the burial of the physical body.

Love showed up in many ways. Food and flowers arrived, and calls came from friends, so many calls that finally someone had to be assigned to the phone to take messages. Many people asked, "What can I do?"

I was in a total fog, but there is one thing I will never forget. Bishop Bill Hamon and his wife, Evelyn, called immediately and offered to fly in the same day to stay with me. That was love to me. It was sacrificial love in action. I needed visible, acted-out love. I pored over every card and letter, and I went through all the phone messages. Just to hear someone's voice spoke volumes to me. Each message was another love download. To this day, I remember those whose love touched me in a remarkable way during that time. They hold a special place in my heart.

Yet it was not an easy week, waiting for the "end." In a time of prayer before Paul's death, I had seen a vision of a beautiful small bird, all alone, sitting in the top of an extremely tall tree. Its little chest jutted out, and it was singing the most beautiful song at the top of its lungs. That bird arrested my attention. All I could do was watch it and listen to it sing.

Then someone brought me this beautiful china bluebird. Another person sent a sympathy card with a picture of that same bird sitting on the top of a tree, singing away. One day while in the master bathroom, I felt grief swallowing me up once again. I felt as though I were going to drown, and I remembered the bird. I fell to my knees and once again began to sing to God. I sang and sang. I sang in English, and I sang in my spiritual language. The more I sang, the deeper the song reached into the core of my heart, my being. Something was happening. I realized this song was coming from the deepest part of me, and it was a love song to Jesus. In the midst of overwhelming pain, I could still sing. And sing I did! Another thread started weaving more of the love tapestry around me in my journey through grief.

Unrelenting Grief

I wish I could tell you that walking out the journey through grief was apple pie and ice cream. It was not. It was one moment at a time, not even one day. One moment I was laughing; the next moment, grief rolled like an angry sea whose temper refused to be calmed. Little did I know that this week in the waiting room was only a sneak preview of what was yet to come. Just because I knew God intimately did not mean I would not go through the valley of the shadow of death. What it did mean was that someone would go with me. And that someone was Jesus.

At times I felt bipolar. Sometimes I would be laughing; other times, crying. If you were there the first time I saw Paul in the casket, you could have heard me wailing from one end of the church to the other. I felt unfathomable heart pain.

Simultaneously, as I looked at him for the first time, I started laughing uncontrollably. I blurted out, "That's not Paul."

It was only his body. Grace began to mantle me like the soft snow of winter to help me navigate the next couple days of viewing and the funeral. It was God's grace. Love began to weave another thread through this new tapestry God was draping over me.

The end came when the funeral was over. That gave finality to Paul's earthly life. My husband's physical body had been lowered into the ground. I would never see him again in this life. I knew intellectually that the real Paul (spirit and soul) was not dead. But from a human perspective, when they lowered the casket into the ground, it was over for me. He was gone. Now I faced the challenge of walking through a season of grief. A walk through the valley alone, by myself.

Journey Toward Recovery

Because Paul's death was sudden, it took a month for the fullness of my new reality to catch up with me. In the first few weeks I told someone, "This is much easier than I thought.

It's like a piece of cake in comparison with what I thought it would be."

I did not realize that I was still in shock, and that the reality of Paul's death had not yet fully caught up with me. Then it settled in. In that long season, grief was my constant companion.

I found several nuggets that helped me get through those months of inexpressible, incomprehensible grief. I made up my mind that I would not try to escape the feelings, but rather would work through them. Having gone through extreme grief as a teenager gave me a grid for what I would have to do. When I was eighteen, in February of my freshman year of college, I lost three of my closest family members to death. My mother committed suicide because of grievous reasons involving a board member of the church. Three weeks later both of my grandparents, with whom I had been very close, died within a day of each other. The loss was so great and so deep that it took me eight years to fully process the grief and work through it. That earlier loss forced me to face life as I never had to before. Suddenly, life was not a bed of roses and I had a cascading series of deaths to work through. Through that experience, I learned what grief felt like and eventually what to do with it—how to work through it.

I was determined to work through it after Paul's death. My doctor offered me tranquilizers or an antidepressant. I said no because it would only numb the feelings and prolong the process. At some point, I would have to face the feelings of loss head-on and plow through them. Now was better than later.

Two other truths were lifesaving for me. First, my husband was not my god. When he died, I still had a future. My husband was not my life; God was. Second, I had a life of my own, a calling from God that would not change. My ministry was not my husband. And it was that call from God that propelled me forward into the future when nothing else did.

Resuming a Semblance of Normalcy

I went back to work as a pastor. That meant I showed up at the office. Productivity was not the issue; getting outside the house was. Being with people made all the difference in the world. I doubt I was very effective or productive. In fact, the emotions of grief were still intense, even while I was in the presence of other people.

By 4 or 5 p.m. every day, I was exhausted. I could not concentrate. I would go home feeling like a mannequin. I could not think, read or talk on the phone. In fact, I could not interact in any way. I would try to read my Bible, and my mind could not even process the words. It would wander aimlessly. I could not sleep, so I watched videos just to focus on something other than the grief. I learned to keep my mind focused, even if it was on something mundane.

I began to travel again a few weeks after the funeral. Something said within me, *Don't give in to retreating.* I listened to that inner nudge. My first trip was to California, and on that trip, the loneliness hit me like a ton of bricks. Staying in a hotel room by myself, it felt like hell on wheels. I would cry myself to sleep, but somehow I still found the grace to minister.

The first place I went, they had planned a huge lunch for all the visiting ministers. I could not handle it. Large gatherings that required interpersonal dialogue only intensified my exhaustion and inability to focus. I asked to eat lunch with a small group instead. I am not sure they understood why, yet they went out of their way to accommodate me. Their acts of kindness were more threads woven into the tapestry of love that surrounded me.

On my second trip, the pastor said he had been in prayer and the Lord had spoken to him about giving me $10,000. He had no idea that I owed that exact amount on the funeral, or that I had no idea how I would come up with that amount of money. Even though the trip was challenging from a personal standpoint, love showed up in one of my darkest moments. Another thread of love was being woven into that tapestry.

It was in that same city that I was so lonely one night that I left my room and wandered the city streets. I knew the city and which areas were safe. I had to get out of my room to keep grief from consuming me.

Saturdays were like days from hell. Before, these had been special days when the two of us worked on things around our home. Since there was no one to work with now, I was totally alone for the first time in years. Because grief can be so all-encompassing, it seemed as though I would never be normal again. I often felt death would be easier than life.

One Saturday was so painful that I could not stop crying. I saw no future, and I felt utterly alone and abandoned. I did not see how God had made a difference at all. *Why had God let my husband die?* I asked myself. *Why did I have to go through this?*

It was more about me now than about my husband. It was about what I had lost and how it felt as if life would never again be happy or normal. I knew I was in trouble.

Then another thread in the tapestry of love showed up. I called a friend and told her what was going on. I was out of control. It so frightened her that she thought I needed medication immediately. She offered to stop by a store and get a bottle of wine so I could drown my sorrows. She did not realize it was her presence I needed.

I told her I did not need something to medicate my pain, just someone present with me. She drove like a maniac over to my house, showing up in her pajamas. What I needed was a real person with me, and the opportunity to pour out my grief. After about an hour of spilling out all the pain, I was okay again.

My friend was love in the flesh, going out of her way to come help me. I knew that the Father cared about my pain; He had sent someone to help me through an impossible place. It was one little step, followed by another little step, helping me shift from grief to the reality that I still had a life to live.

The Battle of Condemnation

Then the next enemy stared me right in the face. At times I would struggle with condemnation because I could not do any sustained Bible reading, study or prayer. I had to preach every Sunday. But by the grace of God, I never missed one Sunday that year. Preparation time meant that with the fifteen to thirty minutes of clarity I had, I received an outline from God and preached from that.

I learned that condemnation did not help, and I could only do what I could do. I learned to give myself grace, even as God was giving me grace.

I also learned that grief is something that has no normalcy to it. It is different with every person, and I had to learn what to do in those impossibly dark moments. I had to come to a place where I accepted the process.

There were nights when I did not know if I would ever see the light of day. The pain was so intense that I felt my heart would burst or break. It felt as if someone had reached into my chest and yanked my heart out—such raw, intense pain. I now understood what it was like to have a broken heart in reality, not just in theory.

One night, the grief was so intense that I did not think I could make it. But love broke through once again. Suddenly, four angels showed up in my room and stood at the four corners of my bed! They lifted me up to a plane where it was as if I had been given a shot of morphine. I was in a realm where I was numbed to the intensity of the pain. I fell asleep and made it through the night. I knew that my Father had sent those angels into my room that night to help me get through it when I could not help myself. He was my Helper!

Prepared Beforehand

All our experiences prepare us for the days ahead. In that preparation is the thread of God's love forming our personal tapestry. I stated earlier that as a teenager, I had lost half of my closest family to death. It took me years to work through that. I became a temporary atheist, and then an agnostic. It was because of that experience that I had cried out to God and experienced a Damascus Road encounter with Jesus. I became enveloped in His incredible love for me. And I began to walk away from all the anger, rage, unforgiveness, bitterness and devastation that had filled my heart and life.

Had I not lost half of my family as a teenager, I would not have had a grid for grief when my husband died. I do not know if I would have made it through as healthily as I did, had it not been for that experience. I was not afraid of the grief because I understood it; I just did not like it. I did not like it at all. It was intensely painful, and it hunted me down day and night. Thankfully, as a young person I had already let go of all the anger, rage and bitterness through several healing encounters with Jesus. Those encounters caused me to know God loved me and deeply cared about me personally. This formed the foundation for walking through the grief of my husband's death. It was the unquestioning love of God that had saved me from a life of unresolved grief and bitterness in my early years.

Several other things also prepared me for this time. Through a unique word from the Lord, I ordered a new car two months before my husband died. The car was due for delivery a week after Paul died, but the day before he died it was delivered a week early. The salesperson also asked if I wanted to buy insurance to pay off the car if anything happened. I explained that my husband had a preexisting condition, so I thought it was improbable that we could be insured. She called the insurance company anyway to check into it, but they were closed for the day. She had us sign the papers anyway, just in case the insurance was valid.

That night, my husband died. Because the papers were filled out and signed, the insurance company had to pay for the car. Not only was the new car totally paid for, but there was also $1,000 extra. My Father knew what was going to happen, and He did not want me driving around in a car that needed help. I had a new car that was paid in full instead.

That was only part of the miraculous preparation. Not only did I have a new car; I also had a new house. Our old house had needed constant repairs. My husband was a real home repair guru. He was the Tim Allen of Shady Oaks (the street we lived on). There wasn't anything he could not fix. But I was nervous. I often wondered about whether, if anything happened to him, I would have a mess on my hands. So we had a new house built and moved into it four months before he died. With a brand-new house, I was totally set up for being alone without having to face repair issues. It was just another indicator of how great God's love for me was, another thread weaving into the tapestry of love around me.

Formed for Love

Eleven months following Paul's death, I slid into a "suddenly." I was standing at the bottom of my stairs in the great room. I had just been in a time of worship where I sang my heart out to God. In that place, once again God lifted me to a plane of absolute and limitless love. I was arrested by Him, captured by Him. It was in that moment that I literally felt grief leave my heart. My chest felt normal again. I could breathe. The feeling that someone was sticking a fist in my chest and ripping out my heart was gone. From that point on, grief was no longer my constant companion.

I continued to experience moments of grief, particularly at holiday times. But the day-in and day-out unrelenting pain was gone. I could say with the psalmist that God delivered me out of all of my afflictions. He also made me lie down in green pastures. He led me beside the still waters. Most of all, He restored my soul. But what did He restore my soul for? He restored it because He loved me. And now, I could reach out to others and walk with them through their hurt and pain.

Grief is not just about losing a loved one. It is about losing anything precious to us. It may be our life as we know it, our physical health, growing older and losing certain abilities and functions, our dream of having a child, a job we love or our dreams for the future. Though each of these things may differ in kind and intensity, each carries an element of grief because something is lost.

In the Bible Job lost everything, yet his latter days following the extreme trauma of grief were greater than the best of his former years. Esther lost her family in war, yet she went on to become queen and save a nation. Perhaps her grief helped her identify even more with her own people group, whose lives were in jeopardy. She had to risk her own life to save them.

Jesus walked through the Garden of Gethsemane, and from there He went to Calvary and lost His life. No one really seemed to care enough to walk with Him through that process except Simon of Cyrene. Then there were the women waiting at His grave. The guys were gone. Those closest to Him had abandoned Him. But Sunday came, when suddenly the grave broke open and He rose triumphant, with a whole new glorified body. He went on to become the ever-present Savior of the world, who could identify with our pain, our weaknesses and our grief.

God's Redemptive Purposes

The Word tells the end of the story. For the joy set before Him, Jesus endured the cross and suffered the shame. Pain is not purposeless. It can lead to greatness, as well as to a deep compassion for those who know pain.

During my season of seemingly unbearable pain and grief, each thread woven into my life wrapped me in a tapestry of love. I was healed to love. I was wrapped in God's personally woven tapestry of love. So are you. Remember, your deepest times of pain can be turned around into your deepest moments when God's love comes shining through. It happened for me. It can happen for you!

Wrapped in His everlasting love,
Barbara J. Yoder

Barbara J. Yoder is the lead apostle and founding pastor of Shekinah Regional Apostolic Center in Ann Arbor, Michigan; and leader of Breakthrough Apostolic Ministries Network, a network of pastors, ministry leaders and marketplace leaders. Information about her ministries is available at http://shekinahchurch.org.

6

There Is Life beyond This Moment

By Doug Stringer

And we know that in all things God works for the
good of those who love him, who have been called
according to his purpose.

Romans 8:28 NIV

Out of our most difficult circumstances, our most painful moments, God desires to bring forth great things. This statement reflects a core value that guides my entire life.

Reflecting on the last three-plus decades of ministry, I am overwhelmed at the goodness of the Lord. I have had the privilege of ministering from the inner city of Houston to numerous parts of the globe. I have also met some amazing people all over the world. My adventures have been many, and my journey full of glorious testimonies. Yet along the way, there have also been those moments when it seemed too difficult, even too painful, to journey on.

One thing I have learned is that every life experience can become a life lesson and part of my life message. In Christ, there is always life for us beyond our moments of challenge, difficulty and pain. This is the nature of God and His love. His love has the final say!

Landmarks from My Early Years

During my high school years in Japan, I was getting ready to wrestle in the Far East Wrestling Championships. I was actually born in Yokosuka, Japan, to a Japanese mother. My father was in the U.S. Navy. He was from Houston, and he was stationed in Japan after the Korean War. He was an Underwater Demolition Team (UDT) frogman (later they became known as Navy SEALS). We moved to San Diego when I was around three years old.

During the Vietnam War, my mother and father divorced, and my mother and stepfather married. My stepfather was also in the navy and was a hospital corpsman. He was from Waco, Texas, so I definitely have lots of Texas roots. When I was in high school, my stepfather was stationed in Japan, which is how I ended up back there.

On the first day of the Far East Wrestling Championships, I fractured my left elbow. My sensei (coach) wrapped my arm and had me put ice on it throughout the night. The next day, he asked me if I wanted to continue in the tournament. Thinking about it for only a brief moment, I decided that my desire to win was greater than my moment of pain. My coach then proceeded to take the bandages off my left arm and put them on my right arm.

I asked him, "Why are you taking those off my hurt arm and putting them on my good arm?"

He simply told me, "Everyone from the day before will remember that you have been injured, but no one will remember which arm."

What followed was like a scene out of the movie *The Karate Kid*, one of those Mr. Miyagi moments. Sure enough, looking for an advantage over me, my opponents went for the arm with the bandages without realizing it was my good arm. Through the pain, I was still able to place second in my weight class that year.

Landmarks like these along the way in my early years have reminded me that there is life beyond our moments of challenge, difficulty and pain. Yet there seems to be little, if anything, more debilitating than a broken heart or wounded spirit. I have had to face those as well.

Turning Points in My Journey

For about two years, starting around 1989, I was in the midst of a difficult time of trials in my life and ministry. I had gone through an emotionally painful period and felt a sense of loss and rejection. I was also being severely harassed and receiving threats (even some death threats) due to some of our ministry outreaches. My car was stolen twice in the space of a few short weeks, right in front of our ministry offices. Vandals also broke in to our offices and did a lot of damage. I was under extreme spiritual, physical and emotional attack.

One time I remember telling my staff and volunteers to leave the offices. I locked the doors, turned off the lights and curled up in a fetal position on the couch in the reception area. I felt numb and spent. I was disillusioned, disappointed and hurt. Quite simply, I felt like giving up.

In that state of heart and mind, I cried out to the Lord, "God, either take me to a people who are truly hungry for You, or take me home to be with You!"

As I mentioned already, nothing is more debilitating than a broken heart or wounded spirit. There were many days I just could not sleep. I could not eat, either, and at times I found it difficult to concentrate. I remember boarding a flight from Houston to Dallas to join Dr. Edwin Louis Cole and Ben Kinchlow for a father-and-son ministry event. I really did not want to go, but out of honor and respect for Dr. Cole, and because he had personally called and requested that I come, I acquiesced.

I had not been able to eat much for nearly two weeks prior. It was not a spiritual fast; I just did not feel like eating. Even the peanuts they offered on the flight repulsed me. I ended up sitting next to a woman who tearfully poured out her heart to me about her life. I sat there with tears in my eyes because of my own hurt, thinking to myself, *Lady, can't you see I have my own problems?* Yet the Lord gave me words of encouragement and comfort for her.

On the flight I sensed the Lord asking me some questions, ones to which many people can relate.

The Lord said to me, *How do you think the people in the world feel who don't have Me? They cover up their despair, pain and rejection with their abuse of drugs, alcohol, promiscuous living and other temporary fixes. They seek to fill the pain and the voids in their hearts with things that will not last. Some even consider ending it all.*

I knew exactly what He was talking about, because I was there. He showed me that if I had not had Him, I would have resorted to those same compensatory facades, trying to compensate on the outside for what I lacked on the inside.

As I pondered my situation, He reminded me, *There is always room for one more at the foot of the cross.*

If the Lord could take care of the hurt, pain and sins of the whole world, then He could take care of what seemed overwhelming to me. He showed me that my healing would come when I reached out to others with His love, out of my own pain.

During that same period, I was invited to speak at a city-wide youth rally to be held at an area high school one evening. Initially I was excited about speaking to this group. But when the time came, I lost interest in going because my heart was still carrying the hurt. I did not want to be around people or even talk to them, much less face an auditorium full of them. But there I was.

As I climbed onto the stage, my heart was heavy. I knew I had to minister the truth of God's Word to those young people, yet at that moment I felt overwhelmed, empty and hardly worthy of bringing the word of the Lord to those who had come with expectant hearts. I was still carrying the weight of a broken heart. That evening, however, was a turning point in my life and ministry. My life experience became my life message. It became the message of God's heart for those whom some label as the directionless generation, as well as for His Church.

The crowd of young people who were present hung on every word I spoke. They seemed to identify with the sense of rejection, pain and heartache I described. To my amazement, a swell of young people came to the front of the auditorium, wanting to dedicate their lives to Christ and walk into their God-given destiny. It was an incredible time.

I had been obedient to go, and in that simple act of obedience, the Lord did what only He can do. I have found that simple obedience is the highest form of worship, especially when done through the crucible of our own experiences.

Out of Pain Came a Life Message

Out of my pain, God was birthing a message of healing and hope that has become a large part of my life message in bringing hope to a fatherless generation. Through that message, books were birthed and movements started in nations around the world to reach a generation that struggles with finding its identity and direction. Recently that message has been a catalyst for me in helping launch the Global Fatherhood Initiative.

On January 2, 1990, I found myself on a flight with a group of Vietnam veterans headed to Vietnam. My longtime friend Roger Helle, a Vietnam veteran himself, was the vice president of Vets With A Mission. Roger was taking this group of vets who had struggled with what some now call PTSD, or posttraumatic stress disorder. He and others had invited me to come along and assist with some humanitarian efforts and ministry on the trip.

In 1990, very few from the West were going into Vietnam. The conditions were oppressive and squalid, and many people were suffering. As we entered Vietnamese airspace, I looked around at our team of fewer than twenty, and I doubt there was a dry eye. I could only imagine the deep reflections, the memories and the pain. Some shared about their struggles with survivor's guilt. Some shared their memories of lost friends. Others shared the nightmare of what they had experienced. Most talked about their postwar struggles. Hearing their stories, their struggles and their pain, as well as seeing the squalid conditions, persecution and poverty of the Vietnamese people, brought clarity and perspective to my life and calling.

When Roger was in Vietnam he, too, experienced a lot of physical and emotional pain. During the war, he was blown up by a hand grenade, shot twice and bayoneted, all in a few moments of time. He suffered multiple shrapnel wounds over his whole body and was physically unrecognizable. The surgeons said he would require numerous operations just to survive.

Roger told me he still remembers the physical and emotional pain he suffered while fighting for his life. To prevent further infection, his wounds had to be scrubbed open each day. He said the pain was so excruciating that he did not think he could bear it. After a while, the infection left and the doctors were able to sew up his physical wounds. Eventually the pain left, and all that remained was a scar and the memories.

Likewise, when we experience emotional pain caused by the wounds of rejection or a broken heart, the memories can seem unbearable. In my case, and likely at some point for you, it seems nearly impossible to overcome. But just as my friend Roger had to go through physical, emotional and spiritual healing, we, too, are being cleansed daily of our wounds, even when the cleansing hurts, so that the Lord can do greater things in and through us.

Out of his experiences, today Roger Helle and his wife direct a very successful Teen Challenge in Chattanooga, Tennessee, bringing healing to the lives of many. They also have an incredible ministry to war veterans. Their ministry touches nations.

During our 1990 trip and subsequent ministry trips, we helped do some work in a polio orphanage and in other orphanages. We also helped build medical clinics, and we served in various social service endeavors. We met with some government officials along the way, as protocol demanded. During one trip, some young Vietnamese Christians approached four of us and asked us to come to a gathering of 125 pastors and church leaders who had been fasting and praying for two weeks in a room in an undisclosed location.

When we arrived, we were humbled by the sacrifices and passion of the heroes of the faith we met. They had suffered much under Communism. One pastor had spent nine years in hard labor reeducation camps because of his faith. Another pastor had been arrested, imprisoned and beaten on numerous occasions. One pastor had just been released from prison the day before, after twelve years at a reeducation camp.

I was humbled when these pastors and leaders asked me to give them a word from the Lord. I thought, *How can I minister to these heroes when I am from a spiritually fat culture that gives up at even slight resistance?*

In my mind, these pastors should have been ministering to us. Nonetheless, they insisted that I share because they believed God had sent us to give them a word of confirmation about what they had been praying for their nation. All I knew to do for the next several hours was to take a basin of water and a towel and wash each of their feet. I also prayed words of knowledge over them.

Some of them could not pronounce my name properly, so they nicknamed me in Vietnamese "the man who washes feet." More than two decades later, I am still in communication with some of these pastors and call them my friends. The Lord has allowed me to serve the Vietnamese community, and I have been invited on many occasions to speak at national and international gatherings with Vietnamese pastors and leaders.

A few years ago, I received a call from another Christian humanitarian organization working in Vietnam, whose founder, Robert, has long been my friend. He was in a coffee shop when some young pastors came up to him and said, "We know America is a very large country, but would you happen to know of a Japanese American named Doug Stringer, whom we know as 'the man who washes feet'?"

Robert responded, "Yes, absolutely, Doug Stringer is a dear and longtime friend."

The pastors seemed excited and told him they had never actually met Doug Stringer, but they had started churches and teachings because of his old videotapes and cassette tapes that are still circulating. Through the Internet, they also had listened to Doug speak at conferences and had used those more recent teachings.

When I look back at the time of deep pain and woundedness I experienced when I was curled up in a fetal position in my office, I see how God's grace abounded and brought about His greater purpose and destiny for nations because I was willing to be a broken vessel for Him.

Your Healing Is in Your Calling

Out of our deepest pains and heartaches, our greatest challenges and our disappointments and discouragements come even greater places of victory and destiny. There is life beyond the moments of pain and challenge. The Holy Spirit comforts us through them, while empowering us with a desire to win that is greater than those moments of pain.

We can draw from a well that never runs dry, because that well comes from the water source that never ceases, the River of Life. The rivers of living water come from the mercy seat of Christ, and His desire is that His rivers flow through each and every one of us. Remember, Jesus said, "He who believes in Me, as the Scripture said, 'From his innermost being will flow rivers of living water'" (John 7:38 NASB). That is an open invitation to every believer.

Who would have thought that my simple obedience to God, pressing on when I did not feel like it, would be used by the Lord to influence people throughout the nations? When His love breaks through, nothing is impossible for God.

A missionary friend of mine and his wife pioneered a great church and many outreaches in South America. They touch many nations, but they went through some very trying times in their early years of ministry. Today he ministers out of the overflow of a love that is more powerful than any realm of darkness. He and his wife are living a life filled with adventure—living the dream—because dreams really do come true. He also reminds us that it was not always easy. In fact, one of the most trying times came when they found out that his wife was diagnosed with cancer.

As they began to seek the Lord and His guidance, to see if they should leave the nation that they love so dearly and come back to the United States, they sensed the Lord saying, *Don't leave your calling to find your healing, for your healing is in the calling.*

May we all live the dream. May we not let discouragement, disappointment or disillusionment distract us from the destinies God has yet to bring forth to the nations. May our desire to win be greater than our moments of challenge, difficulty and pain. There is life beyond the moment. Our hope and healing are in our calling!

For me, this is part of what love looks like. It includes the implanting of an eternal life perspective in our hearts, that *there is life beyond this moment.*

With faith, hope and love,
Doug Stringer

Doug Stringer is a revivalist at heart. He is founder and president of Turning Point Ministries International, which gave birth to a global movement and network of ministries. Information about his ministry is available at http://somebodycares.org and http://www.dougstringer.com.

7

Don't Let Pain Have the Final Say

By Joan Hunter

But as for you, you meant evil against me; but God meant it for good. . . .

Genesis 50:20 NKJV

Telling my personal story now has a divine purpose—to encourage you and others to hang on to and believe in God's plan and purpose for your life. Giving you hope and building up your faith is truly worth all I went through. I have gone through multiple low valleys in my life, but with His grace and love, God has broken through all the stuff of the past. He has restored everything in Jesus.

I could easily have given up, but I did not. If you are at a point in your life where you are considering throwing in the towel and giving up, I have a word for you: God has great plans for you—plans to turn your life around. Get ready for an awesome rest of your life!

A Rough and Tough Beginning

Before I took my first breath, my father abandoned my mother. I came forth into the world and grew up not knowing my earthly father. Soon after starting school, I was diagnosed with a serious learning disability. My mother worked long hours to provide for my brother and me. Often we would dig in garbage cans to find bits of fruit to eat. My early days measured far below what is considered a normal childhood.

Many days while growing up, I felt as though I were living in hell, and I knew there was nothing I could do about it. But I did know God. I knew Jesus lived within me. Still, my forward progress through life was one intense battle for me from an early age.

Charles Hunter joined our family on January 1, 1970, when he married my mother, Frances. We then moved from Florida to Houston, Texas. Charles had a big heart and quickly adopted me. At sixteen years of age, I finally had a dad. He was wonderful, and we had a great relationship. Finally, my life was getting better.

Then I met a man at Oral Roberts University in 1972, and I married him two years later. We traveled with my parents the Happy Hunters, Charles and Frances, for the next several years. We started a church in Dallas, and life was good. I had a gifted and talented husband who was serving God. We were working together toward an incredible life.

God blessed us with four beautiful daughters who were the bright spots of every day. Being a natural nurturer, I easily extended that gift to include not only my girls, but all my friends and church members. A beautiful home, our wonderful daughters, co-pastoring a church and traveling part-time with my parents as international healing evangelists kept my life challenging, interesting and very busy. We were living our dream.

Then Everything Exploded . . .

Throughout those years, however, something seemed to block our progress. We stood on the edge of promotion so often, but as a married couple we just could not take that next step. Yet my husband, who was also my pastor, could not identify any problems that might be holding us back.

I called out to God, "Why is this happening to our family? Is there anything in my life that is unpleasing to You? Please reveal it to me. I want to be sold out for You, Jesus! I want to be used by You. I want to be blessed. I want to do all I can do for You."

Instead of progressing upward, we plummeted in the opposite direction, into debt and confusion. Doors that looked open and inviting slammed shut in our faces. Life became a battle all over again. I sought God's face daily, and I heard nothing in return. We both took secular jobs in order to keep finances coming into our home.

Then the bomb exploded. God drew back the curtain and revealed that my husband was living an alternative lifestyle, his hidden secret. After 25 years of marriage, my life was shattered! We lost the church. My beautiful home was sold to pay the bills. Shocked by the devastating news, my friends scattered in reaction to the trauma. They did not know what to say or do to help me because they were also hurting.

My children were equally hurt and confused—their father, their friend, their pastor was not the person they had believed him to be. How could he have hidden this unbelievable secret from everyone?

This man was the moneymaker and provider in our household. Along with my relationship with the Lord, my husband had been my security for 25 years. As it turned out, he did not need me for anything, while I had depended on him for everything. He was the decision maker and leader of our home, family and church. I was a seriously codependent follower. I had spent my time trying to please and take care of everyone else—him, our home, our children, friends and church members.

How am I to survive now? I asked myself. We had three girls in college. *Will the girls be able to finish school?* I wondered. *Without our church and family structure, who am I? Do I have a future? Why has all this happened?*

Pain, Pain, Everywhere!

To say I fell to my knees in utter anguish is putting it mildly. I could not stand, I could not see, I could not think, I could not understand, I could not move. For months, all I felt was pain—the pain of betrayal, the pain of devastation, the pain only a totally broken heart can cause. My heart had been brutally ripped out of my chest, run through a shredder, stomped on until it was an unrecognizable blob of flesh and then buried deep within me. My heart just could not do its job; it could not function. I could not function. I walked in a fog, numbly putting one foot in front of the other.

I had no desire to eat or drink, even though my intellect told me I had to eat to survive. Did I want to survive and face another day of pain and agony? No! I desperately wanted the nightmare to end.

My earthly father had abandoned me, my husband was gone, my children were now grown and three of them were out of the house, my home was gone, the church was gone and most of my friends were now absent from my life. My support system had disappeared. I felt so abandoned and alone.

The sun shone down brightly from the heavens over the Dallas skyline, but it might as well have been midnight, with a violent thunderstorm raging. I recognized little and responded to less. Gone were my bright eyes and welcoming smile. My glowing personality had shriveled up and buried itself under mounds of pain and destruction. Even though I knew God was eternally faithful, I could not see what He was doing in this situation. The pain utterly blinded me.

My take-home pay from a secular job at an automotive company was $1,200 a month. With a house payment of $1,100, I knew that realistically I could not make it on my own. After giving my tithes to God, I was already at a negative balance. What was I to do? Texas does not award alimony, and the children were too old for child support. My departed husband had a great secular job, but legally he had no responsibility to care for his family, so he did very little. It was devastating.

After studying my finances at length, my CPA advised me to stop tithing and giving offerings. He told me to plan on filing bankruptcy because he saw no way for me to make it financially. I quickly cut off those words in Jesus' name and released him. I would not accept such negative words. No one would convince me to stop giving to God.

Counselors told me that I would never get over the emotional trauma. I was experiencing nine out of the ten stressors considered most destructive to someone's life. They told me it would take me seven or eight years to feel better, and that I would probably never fully recover. Everyone I talked to spoke more doom and gloom into my life.

Two days after the divorce was final, I had a sonogram that showed my left breast was filled with a large, dark mass. I could hear the nails being pounded into my casket. In my mind, I was choosing how I would be dressed for my funeral.

The lies from the enemy multiplied exponentially as I prepared to die. No more embarrassment. No more tears. Finally, I would be free from pain. In heaven, I would be truly free. I could dance and sing and worship God. I would not have to face misery and pain again.

What Do I Do?

Coming back to reality, I realized I had four great reasons to live—Charity, Spice, Melody and Abigail—my four remarkable daughters. Slowly, I started to eat again. I took one bite for Charity, one for Spice, one for Melody and one for Abigail. Only their faces before me could encourage me to open my mouth and take just one more bite of food.

I felt as though the big "D" for divorce was tattooed across my forehead. I wanted so desperately to serve God, but divorced people are not exactly welcome in church leadership or ministry—especially a divorced woman!

Where can I go to serve Him? I wondered. *Who will allow me to do anything in their church?*

I sold whatever I could to keep food on the table and pay the bills. No one ever went hungry. The necessities of life would appear out of nowhere . . . gifts on the front steps, money in the mailbox, food deliveries to fill up the cupboards and refrigerator. God supplied our needs again and again.

Each night would find me in my shower, wailing aloud to God. The only one on earth who witnessed the sight or heard my woeful cries was my faithful dog, also confused by recent events.

Night after night, I wailed, "God, You don't have any idea how badly I hurt! I can't make it through this. You haven't any idea how much this heart, this mind and this body hurt!"

One night, in His beautiful still, small voice, I heard God say, *You think I don't know? Yes, I do. I had to turn My back on My*

*own Son on the cross for you, so that you wouldn't have to bear
this pain. I know what pain is. I know the pain you're feeling.*
I apologized, "Father, forgive me. You do understand the
pain I'm going through, but only You can take this pain away."

Inch by Inch

I would love to say my healing was instantaneous; however, it
was not. Inch by inch, I crawled out of that pit into His loving
arms. God carefully reached deep within me, took my bleeding heart, molded it into a brand-new one and gently placed it
back into my chest to function at 100 percent.

God healed me of broken-heart syndrome—a disease where
the heart muscles shred on the inside. Today, my heart is better
than normal! He filled me with His love, His peace, His joy,
His forgiveness and His mercy. He healed me inside and out
and then sent me to share that same possibility of healing with
everyone I meet around the world.

I knew that I knew that I was loved by my God. I was not
dumb, stupid and worthless. God wanted me for Himself! I might
have been abandoned by two men, but my God was always with
me, holding me and collecting all my tears (see Psalm 56:8). He
heard my cries and saw my heart. Pleasing people was no longer
important to me because pleasing God was my ultimate joy.

The peace I sought was in His arms, in His Presence. The
arms of man fell helplessly short in comparison. What I had
sought in other people and the things of the earth were found
only in my heavenly Father, His precious Son, Jesus, the Holy
Spirit and the relentless love of God. Nothing could compare
to His design, His world and His love.

Satan tried to destroy me so many times through the years.
For instance, he meant the growth in my breast to kill me and
annihilate God's plan for my life.

I could easily have given in and given up, but God stepped in, drew a line in the sand and said, "Satan, this far and no more! You will not have this life! I have chosen her to spread My healing message around the world. She is Mine!"

During that time in my life I went after God, asking Him to heal my heart. I knew surgeons could remove the breast and I could live, but I could not live with a broken heart. When I got free of the worry, betrayal, trauma, abandonment, resentment, anger, unforgiveness and the like, then the growth supernaturally disappeared. I was no longer feeding it with negative emotions.

With the cards stacked against me in every area of life—physically, mentally, emotionally and financially—the world offered no hope. I heard the words "You will never recover!" so often when I looked to human help—doctors, counselors and an accountant. Certainly they could give me educated answers, or so I had thought, and they might be good to turn to. Yet they could do nothing in my situation.

I refused to let the enemy steal another seven or eight years of my life, and I cried out to God, "This is my covenant with You! Heal me!"

He answered me. He healed me. Life began again. I could truly say, "But as for you, you meant evil against me; but God meant it for good, in order to bring it about as it is this day, to save many people alive" (Genesis 50:20 NKJV).

Over time, God healed me in every area of my life. He has blessed me with an incredible home, incredible health, an incredible family and a wonderful, caring husband. God has blessed me financially. Everything that was lost, He has restored.

Ministering to hurting people is now my passion. Healing the physical body is important, but healing the soul and spirit is also vital to someone's total restoration. God is a God of restoration. He does not just hand out a Band-Aid to cover something up. He replaces broken hearts, He removes the scars,

He resurrects dead bodies. Yes, He restores finances and blesses His kids with new life. He blessed my girls with scholarships beyond what we could have asked for.

God's Restorative Love

Talk about pure love—God has no ulterior motive or agenda. He wants His best for me, His child. To accept His will and enjoy His gifts and blessings, I simply had to obey Him and position myself to receive. Accepting His gifts and blessings was not the final step, however. Walking in the fullness of His gifts was enormously important, or His blessings would have dissipated and gone down the drain. It was important that I be renewed in the spirit of my mind (see Romans 4:23). As Romans 12:2 (NKJV) says, "And do not be conformed to this world, but be transformed by the *renewing of your mind*, that you may prove what is that good and acceptable and perfect will of God" (emphasis added).

Currently, I travel the world to share my amazing, inspiring story with thousands of hurting people who are searching for what I have already found. In addition, the details of my spiritual walk and my accomplishments always stun the professional community. I was told early in life that I could never accomplish anything and that I would probably never read or write due to my learning disability. Today, not only am I healed, but God also has given me teachings, insights and books to help others. In every teaching, I share the revelations God has given me through the years. At this moment I have fourteen books in print, most of them translated into several languages. The written word travels around the world into areas I cannot physically reach.

Testimonies of miracles frequently come in from those who read and use my books. I am amazed by God's restorative love. God is still using that little girl who was told she would probably never be able to read or write. I am so grateful for every redemptive opportunity. Miracles happen daily as we touch others—in person, through the written word, over the Internet, on TV or on the phone lines. God moves in so many different ways when we willingly allow Him to use us.

> The Spirit of the LORD is upon Me, because He has anointed Me to preach the gospel to the poor; He has sent Me to heal the brokenhearted, to proclaim liberty to the captives and recovery of sight to the blind, to set at liberty those who are oppressed.
>
> Luke 4:18 NKJV

It took a few years before I discovered God's assignment for me—His purpose for my birth. I thought I wanted man's approval, when I truly only wanted or needed His. Only God could choose crumpled-up Joan out of the masses of people and guide me, love me and turn me into one of His spokeswomen to travel and teach for Him. I am daily desperate for Him because I cannot live without my heavenly Father.

By the grace of God, I have now ministered in more than forty countries over the past forty years. Telling my story and ministering His healing love to the sick and hurting never gets old. As tears of happiness run down their faces, my own tears remind me so often of God's goodness and love. Only He could have gotten me through all those lonely nights. Only He could heal me and truly restore me to new life.

God Can Turn It All Around

Now it is your turn. If your life is in chaos right now, get help— the right kind of help. Plug in to God's Spirit living within you. You can operate with His love, His wisdom and His understanding. Give everything to Him. Know that your *cannot* will become His *can*. "For 'who has known the mind of the LORD

that he may instruct Him?' But we have the mind of Christ"
(1 Corinthians 2:16 NKJV).

My advice to you? Cut off the negative words spoken over
you and your situation. Stay in God's Word. Praise His Name
daily. Walk in His Presence. Be obedient to His voice. Seek His
face. Listen to Him. Give Him everything in your life. Follow His
peace. Worship Him with all your heart, mind and soul. Find
Spirit-filled people who can counsel you, advise you, instruct
you and encourage you. Command the trauma to leave your
heart and body. Completely forgive those who have hurt you.
God does not want just to heal your heart . . . He will remove
the sting of your past bad memories. As He said in Isaiah 43:25
(NKJV), "I, even I, am He who blots out your transgressions for
My own sake; and I will not remember your sins." And in Philippians 3:13 (NKJV), Paul says, "But one thing I do, forgetting
those things which are behind and reaching forward to those
things which are ahead."

Turn to God, curl up in His arms and allow Him to heal
you. Allow God's plans to move you into the perfect position
to receive all He has for you. I made it, and you can, too! Let
God take your mess and turn your life around. "And the peace
of God, which surpasses all understanding, will guard your
hearts and minds through Christ Jesus" (Philippians 4:7 NKJV).

Not only did God heal me; now I minister with greater compassion, knowing what others are going through. Isaiah 61 is
the embodiment of God's call on my life. I truly believe this is
the call of God on your life also. This is the picture of a journey
from devastation into His perfect will. This is His plan for us
all. Read it out loud. Declare it as His prophetic Word. Speak
it over yourself and your life, and then walk it out with Him
beside you.

God is not a respecter of persons. He turned my mourn-
ing into dancing. His amazing love broke through my years

of trauma, and He wants to do the same for you. Rejoice with me, and praise Him. Do not let pain have the final say. If God is on your side, then you are a winner, too!

Expecting God's love to break through for you,
Joan Hunter

Joan Hunter is devoted to equipping believers through the 4 Corners Conference Center in Tomball, Texas, to take the healing power of God beyond the four walls of the church to the four corners of the earth. She is the founder and president of Joan Hunter Ministries. Information about her ministry is available at http://www.joanhunter.org.

8

Love Rescued Me

By Harry R. Jackson Jr.

For He *rescued* us from the domain of darkness, and
transferred us to the kingdom of His beloved Son.

Colossians 1:13 NASB, emphasis added

Have you ever felt like giving up? No, I am not talking
about suicide per se. I am speaking of suffering a devastating feeling of defeat and personal loss. Has it ever
seemed as though you are on a downward spiral that cannot
be stopped? Have you ever had event after event occur in your
life, making you believe the "good old days" are over?

I would like to share with you a step-by-step approach to
discovering the love of God and activating His mercy, grace and
majesty in our lives. I will do this through sharing a testimony
about an ordeal that my family and I endured and survived. But

our story is more than a testimony; it also contains scriptural help for others struggling to make sense of long-term trials.

These Very Things Happened to Me

About nine years ago, I was diagnosed with a virulent strain of cancer. I was given only a 10 to 15 percent chance of surviving the attack. After beating the original diagnosis of esophageal cancer, I began a slow, arduous trek to survival and recovery.

Much to my surprise, my wife of over 37 years, Vivian, was also diagnosed with cancer just two and a half years after my diagnosis. I was not fully out of the woods when we got the word about my wife. That put a great deal of pressure on our daughters. Imagine first seeing your dad lose over 75 pounds and barely escape death, and then almost as quickly, seeing your mother develop a rare blood cancer.

A little over five years ago, I visited my wife in a celebrated hospital in downtown Baltimore. She had just gone through a sophisticated adult stem cell transplant procedure in which her own stem cells were used. The procedure is called an autologous stem cell transplant, or a blood or marrow transplant. Her bone marrow had stopped working and was not producing enough healthy stem cells. A blood cancer condition called multiple myeloma was the cause of her difficulty, and a stem cell transplant was prescribed to help her body make enough healthy white and red blood cells, and platelets. Essentially, doctors gave her an infusion of healthy stem cells to replace her damaged and diseased stem cells.

I will never forget getting off the elevator on my way to Vivian's room and having to go through an entry area that was designed to keep patients free from the germs of the outside world. Hermetically sealed doors separated this special section from the other rooms on the floor. In this super-clean area, I remember praying with my wife and asking the Lord to give us a miracle.

Believe it or not, walking through my wife's illness as her caregiver was more stressful than being sick myself. I struggled to be the breadwinner, pillar of strength and leader I thought everyone wanted me to be. When I was diagnosed, I moved into a unique fighting mode, and I never really doubted that our God would have the final say in my situation. With my wife's diagnosis and my household involved, I had a much harder time shifting into a faith mode. When Vivian was diagnosed, I suddenly felt helpless. I felt an overwhelming sense of pressure. I had not even realized how reassuring it was to wake up during my hospital stays and see her face during the 24 months of my illness. But when my wife became ill, I temporarily lost my joy and perspective. I was bewildered and a little disoriented.

Suffice it to say that our consecutive bouts of cancer put our whole family on an emotional roller coaster. This created a whirlwind of negative activity around us. For a myriad of reasons, we lost nearly half of our three-thousand-plus congregation and millions of dollars of annual ministry income. We also felt abandoned by many longtime friends and admirers.

One minister explained the phenomenon like this: "Often a minister's congregation does not love him. Rather, they love his gift."

It is also a truism to declare that if your primary gifts no longer function at full strength, you can suddenly lose your sphere of authority, and your career will seemingly spiral downward.

To sum it all up, my wife, Vivian Michele, and I nearly lost our lives. We could have lost our marriage, we nearly lost our ministry and we nearly lost our ministry's buildings and lands. But Jesus allowed us to begin a resurrection process.

We believed that our God had not forsaken us. We believed He still loved us. Even though we did not understand how these compounded troubles had reached our doorstep, we chose to trust His love.

Turning On the Light of Hope

Sometimes public figures cannot conquer their private demons of drug or alcohol addiction and seemingly "fall from grace and prominence." This kind of downturn in momentum and effectiveness is not just the purview of aging actors, singers or other public figures, though. After seven years of fighting one uphill health challenge after another, I began to look for a place where I could turn in my resignation from life, ministry and public engagement. But somehow the Lord broke in on me, and His love chased me down in a very definite way. So in this chapter, I am giving you a combination—my testimony of how Jesus' powerful love intervened in my shattered world, plus biblical truths that you can follow like stepping-stones across the perilous waters in your life. Isaiah 43:2–3 (KJV) expresses the Lord's desires for you and me:

> When thou passest through the waters, I will be with thee; and through the rivers, they shall not overflow thee: when thou walkest through the fire, thou shalt not be burned; neither shall the flame kindle upon thee. For I am the LORD thy God, the Holy One of Israel, thy Saviour.

Our Lord desperately wants to reveal Himself to us. The primary image He used to describe Himself in the Old Testament was the image of a shepherd. In the New Testament, He takes the disclosure of His character to another level by revealing Himself to mankind as our heavenly Father. If you are facing a nearly hopeless situation, you must remember that everything starts with hope. The Lord wants to shepherd each of us personally, positively and powerfully. He also wants to reveal His fatherhood to each of us. We can turn on the light of hope by asking Him to make Himself known in our lives and help us experience His love in action.

The first lesson I learned in my ordeal was that I had to postpone giving up. I have jokingly told audiences around the country, "I made myself wait to give up until tomorrow!" I usually go on to say, "I never found out whom to turn my resignation in to!"

The truth is that our whole family soldiered through our difficulties until we learned how to cooperate with God's grace. We all learned that our attitude and faith would determine how we react to our problems. From the earliest diagnosis to the greatest ordeals, we have continued to grow in the knowledge of God. If you have been close to giving up, come grow with me as I tell you the rest of our story.

The Reason for Jesus' Miracles

In the gospel of John, Jesus declared that He only did what He saw the Father doing (see John 5:19). When we see Jesus performing the seven miracles that John recorded, He therefore was revealing the character of the Father through these works of power. His compassion and love were the primary motivators behind these miracles. The almighty, omniscient God revealed His trustworthiness and love to us in the gospel of John. He still identifies with the needs of people in our world today.

As my wife and I journeyed from despair to hope, we needed several major miracles. The Scriptures became the vehicle through which God spoke to us to frame our thoughts, expectations and experiences. When the Lord desires to perform transformational miracles in our lives, He often entices us into an attitude of faith. We saw that every one of the miracles in

John was motivated by the Lord's compassion and love. As we look at those seven miracles from Scripture, let me share with you how Vivian and I have learned to cooperate with God's desire to bring miracles into all our lives.

Miracle #1

It was love that turned water into wine at a family wedding (see John 2:3–10).

The day of my endoscopy, the test that revealed a cancerous tumor the size of a golf ball in my esophagus, I realized in my morning devotional that I had cancer. I cannot explain exactly how I knew. I just knew—deep within me. I also knew that Jesus would be with me in the ordeal.

After the test, the examining doctor told me that they could not finish the test and that my family doctor would explain what they had found. This was not the good news I was hoping for. But I realized that the God whose presence I sensed in my morning prayer knew that I had cancer long before the doctors knew, or before I knew.

I realized what I think the bridal couple in the gospel of John experienced. Jesus' first miracle was an expression of empathy and compassion. By turning water into wine at a wedding, He kept one Jewish family from social ridicule and embarrassment. The wedding was a big deal for them and their circle of friends. For the bride especially, the wedding represented a major milestone in her life. In light of this, Jesus' action declared His concern for everyday people. Our Lord was not just showing His support and endorsement of marriage. He was showing His ongoing commitment to that man and his wife. It was as though our God was saying, "I promise to be an overshadowing influence in your marriage and family life from this moment forward. You will never be alone again!"

In my health ordeal, I discovered that Jesus wanted to protect me from harm. As He had with the wedding party in that miracle, I realized Jesus wanted to get personal and involved with me. He wanted to bail me out of trouble. He used His power to heal me spiritually and physically, and to protect me from ridicule.

Miracle #2

It was love that healed the royal official's son in Capernaum (see John 4:46–54).

One day I went to the hospital for my typical blood draw and oncological appointment. I suddenly passed out and fell on the floor as the technician was drawing my blood. My entire right side went limp, and I temporarily lost the ability to speak. What a scary feeling!

As the hospital staff lifted me from the floor, I realized that this episode was not a dream. I was sicker than I could ever have imagined. Weeks of chemotherapy and radiation treatments had weakened my system. Little did I know that the deacon who had driven me to the hospital called my church immediately. Within minutes of my stroke, hundreds of people had begun to pray. Ninety minutes or so after I fainted, the stroke symptoms disappeared and I came back to myself. The doctors were amazed at my rapid recovery; nonetheless, I had to remain in the hospital for three days as they pondered my condition.

The news of my survival gave me an opportunity to preach to everyone in my sphere of influence about the faithfulness of God. Through my suffering, my trust in God was being deepened. Despite the master trial of cancer, God demonstrated that He "had the devil on a leash," as I like to say.

The miracle of the royal official's son shows how our faith can actually grow during an ordeal. A desperate father at his wit's end came to Jesus, who was his only hope of seeing his son raised up from an incurable disease. This wealthy man had only secondhand knowledge of Jesus. Jesus challenged him to believe a simple statement: "Go thy way; thy son liveth" (John 4:50 KJV).

Jesus made no big production of the healing; He just made a matter-of-fact declaration. The desperate father came in hope, but left in faith. Everyone promises to live for God—after they receive their sought-after miracle. They promise to do great works in exchange for their deliverance. (This is called negotiating with God.) But if the Lord does not perform the miracle the way they expect, they often give up and go home. The Lord gave this nobleman a personal directive, and the man chose to act on it in faith.

Like the nobleman, I learned that Jesus intervenes in our affairs as He chooses. At the end of the story, this nobleman went back home and preached to his large household, family and estate staff. He became a firsthand witness of the power of God. In my life as well, I was able to speak to the people around me in my family, in the hospital, in my church and in the community.

The Lord does not create problems such as Vivian and I were having, but He can rescue us because of His mercy. As He reveals His power and lifts us out of trouble, we have an opportunity to share the character of our God with others. On the one hand, our family and friends may argue with our theology and worldview. On the other hand, they cannot refute our simple testimony of how God moved.

Miracle #3

Love healed the paralyzed man at Bethesda in a way that prevented relapse (see John 5:1–18).

As my cancer treatments continued, I had several major conversations with family members. After weeks of meditation about my life and destiny, I announced to my eldest daughter that I believed I would be a winner whether I survived cancer or not. I told her that if Jesus was going to allow me to die and go to heaven, I had nothing to fear and nothing to lose. For a Christian, heaven is a promotion. On the other hand, I reassured her that if my work was not done here on earth, I could count on healing and recovery.

Strangely, from that conversation on I had a growing conviction that I would recover. Along with the growing sense that God was not through with me, I also sensed the Lord dealing with me about character flaws and secret sins in my life. What inner agony! I started thinking about things I would do differently, if given another chance. The biggest problems I faced had to do with pride and presumption. Overall, I had not been thankful for the blessings God had given me.

In this third miracle, Jesus arrived at Bethesda, where many people awaited healing. He approached a group of "disabled" people, including the blind, lame and paralyzed. Among them was a man who had been crippled for 38 years.

Jesus asked this man the craziest question: "Do you want to be healed?" It was as though He was implying that the man had a choice about whether he would remain disabled or choose to move into health. Jesus eventually told the man to rise up, roll up his mat and go and sin no more.

It seems to me that the Lord was saying this man's personal sin would keep him from fully overcoming his disability. Love, not nitpicking, was why Jesus pointed out to the man the trap of continued sin he could find himself in. Love was why Jesus told him to go and sin no more.

The man knew exactly what Jesus was talking about. A heavenly guardrail was erected, and Jesus gave Him restorative direction.

That is exactly what happened to me. As I pursued my physical healing, the Lord required me to address iniquities (character problems and sin patterns) in my life. Pride, fear, insensitivity to others, carnality and presumption were just a few areas in which the loving light of Jesus exposed darkness in me.

For me, repentance was the process of agreeing with God, turning from my inner "moral disability" and then humbly receiving God's empowering grace to overcome. Until the grace kicked in, I had to exercise willpower, resist personal temptation to say or do the wrong thing and focus on learning new attitudes and actions.

Miracle #4

Jesus' love compelled Him to feed five thousand hungry people (see John 6:5–14).

I will never forget my first meeting with my surgeon. This man removed a tumor the size of a golf ball, reconstructed my digestive system and oversaw the nearly eight-hour surgery. As the department head of one of the nation's finest teaching hospitals, he was bright, upbeat and full of energy. He announced to my wife and me the exact statistical probability of my survival, both from the intense presurgery treatment protocol and from the surgery itself. With that, he almost turned that beautiful Saturday morning in Maryland into a moment of fear and foreboding. At the end of our meeting, we asked if it would be okay to take a short family vacation before I began the cancer treatments.

Part of me wanted to save money and prepare for the crisis of the treatments to come. Part of me knew that my family needed an upbeat memory. We also needed to feed our faith by studying the Word of God, refresh our spirits by fellowshiping with dear friends and give thanks to the Lord for His faithfulness.

Our family vacation was phenomenal, "just what the doctor ordered." It became the spiritual highlight of our year. We attended a Christian conference called "The Gathering of Champions" in England. We got special discount tickets to London, booked an awesome hotel with room service and attended the conference, which had become a tradition for us.

At one of the services, a guest speaker stopped and prayed a special prayer for us—without knowing the ordeal we were facing. His prayer centered on the Lord meeting our financial needs in the days ahead. That conference prayer reminds me of the instance of Jesus providing food for the crowd in this fourth miracle. This was not a miracle of desperation. The Lord's power was manifested so that this spiritually hungry crowd could continue to hear His teaching without having to journey back home to eat. Was this an unnecessary use of Jesus' power? Or did Jesus make a simple value judgment that feeding our spiritual man is also necessary for our survival?

As I meditated on this Scripture, I saw the forethought and interventional planning that is in the heart of God. When folks prioritize feeding their spirit man, they are seeking God's Kingdom. Some of these people in John 6 could ill afford to pay for even a short out-of-town excursion and an extra meal, yet they came. Although their trip was not international, it was out of their comfort zone. Jesus generously showed the Father's heart of love, concern and thoughtfulness for them. He created a community memory filled with healings, miracles and family unity.

Time and time again in our family's years of challenges and calamities, we saw Jesus' provision financially and materially. Physical healing, financial provision and timely intervention into our affairs are all part of the Lord's commitment to be with each of our families as we walk through seasons of difficulties. He is not just with us in church. He is with us in the pit. And most importantly, He is with us as we are climbing out of dark places.

Miracle #5

Love compelled Jesus to rescue His friends from a terrifying storm by walking to them on the water (see John 6:16–21).

As my illness went through its stages, my troubles intensified. First, my wife contracted blood cancer. Next, I was hospitalized with pneumonia on two occasions after my wife became ill. On top of all this, I took unpopular positions on local and national moral issues, which caused many local church people to label me as "a little too radical" and "a little too political." We lost scores of members after I decided to launch a national pro-biblical marriage campaign. Unfortunately, many folks considered our activities purely political.

In the whirlwind of facing the extremes of growing popularity on a national level and, at the same time, increased persecution on a personal level, my family and I had to find inner peace and peace with God. To compound matters, my moral stance cost us friends, partners and financial supporters. Some Republican donors thought I was not aggressive enough. Some even saw my biblical emphasis on marriage as political compromise, while many of my black Democratic friends felt I had "sold out" my own race. More specifically, attacking President Obama's social policies made me a cultural pariah in some circles.

Several of my messages went viral and were celebrated by Christians all over the United States, but many of my local members felt betrayed. Some of my former members wrongly thought that I was receiving huge personal funding for speaking the way I was. As a result of all of the racial and cultural turmoil, I began bleeding both people and finances at the local church level. What a turn of events! What a reward for taking a strong biblical position!

In my personal life, Jesus came walking into my church situation at just the right moment. He orchestrated the sale of underutilized properties as a way of solving our financial problems, and He helped us initiate a rebranding strategy for our ministry. Simultaneously, the cancer troubling my wife went into remission, and she was finally awarded the doctorate in education that she had been working on for ten years.

I felt very much like the disciples when Jesus came walking to them on the water. One moment they felt overwhelmed and bewildered. The next moment, He walked upon the water *just to comfort His disciples in the middle of a terrible storm.* Jesus had sent these men to their next ministry assignment, but a huge storm had attempted to take them off course.

It is important for us all to remember that there will be moments in which we feel that something will take us out of the will of God. Often, when there is no sign of Jesus' presence with us, He is actually watching from afar, and He is planning how He will join us in our struggle.

This is similar to how natural mothers work. When my two daughters were young, my wife trained her ears to listen for their footsteps. Even when they could not see her, she knew exactly where they were all night. If they got out of bed, she could tell which one was walking and how far they went. Whenever necessary, she would rise and go to their rescue, or swoop in and bring correction. They may have felt alone at times, but a vigilant parent was always a few steps ahead of them.

Miracle #6

Jesus' love led Him to heal a man born blind so that the man could fulfill his destiny and give God the glory (see John 9:1–7).

One Tuesday, I drove my wife to her doctor's office. She was going for an infusion scheduled to last about ninety minutes.

The traditional blend of chemo given to blood cancer patients had caused her to go bald and had released wave after wave of nausea. Vivian was named after her aunt, who we think died at a much more advanced age of the same kind of blood disorder. I felt sorry for Vivian because I had experienced my share of dry heaves, light-headedness and fatigue during my cancer treatments. Also, I realized that she did not get to choose her genetic predisposition toward multiple myeloma.

Little did I know, however, that Vivian was receiving a new drug that day. As a result of the new medication, Vivian had an allergic reaction. According to the doctor, she nearly died. Later on, the doctor said that "something told her" to check on Vivian 45 minutes or so earlier than normal. Of the miniscule number of people who had allergic reactions to that medicine, a huge number of them had died.

Just like the man born blind in this sixth miracle, Vivian's genetic predisposition toward cancer was a setup for divine intervention. Ultimately, her healing and growing strength tells the world of the goodness of our God.

Miracle #7

It was Jesus' love for Lazarus and his family that made Jesus wait until Lazarus had been dead for four days before raising him from the dead (see John 11:1–45).

Seven years after my original cancer diagnosis, I was told that the doctors had damaged my heart during radiation treatments. More specifically, the treatments had weakened the left side of my heart. Late Saturday night during the last week of June 2013, I concluded that I was very sick. I decided not to go to the emergency room that Saturday, so I waited until Sunday morning. When I finally got to the hospital, the doctors watched over me until early Monday morning. It was hard to believe that I had nearly died again. The diagnosis was congestive heart failure.

My wife, doctors and closest friends kept asking me why I had pushed myself so hard during my obviously slow recovery over that eight-year period. I, on the other hand, wondered why the Lord had not lifted me out of my whirlwind of troubles sooner. Why did Jesus let so many good people leave my church? My budget had dropped by millions of dollars in just a two-and-a-half-year period.

The fall after my heart problems, as I reflected on my financial, spiritual and physical weakness, I felt that the Lord told me He had sent away people who were not joined to our current vision. A couple of Bible stories passed through my mind, one of which was the story of Gideon's valiant three hundred men. This remnant had the right character and spiritual authority to retake important spiritual ground, and then win new natural ground as well by the empowerment of the Lord.

Needless to say, like the family of Lazarus, I felt that the Lord's delay was something of a rejection. The timing of God's intervention bewildered and confused me. There seemed few talented people to lean on. I also had little strength to turn things around.

I had always been a very hands-on leader. I needed to work with a team, empower others and trust the work of the Holy Spirit in the lives of my members. Practically, this meant I needed a stronger middle-management team to turn my organizational mess around. I also realized that I had four levels of death working in me:

1. A wounded spirit—I had to admit that I was offended and hurt.
2. Unprocessed grief—I needed to work through my sense of loss.

3. Unforgiveness—I needed to release and let go of how I felt about people who had betrayed and wronged me.

4. Shame—I had to cast off my feelings of shame, while acknowledging that I had done some things wrong.

Looking back, it seems to me that until I dealt with these four issues in my life, I was unable to sustain a hopeful, joyful attitude. Jesus seemingly let every false hope fail me. Similarly, He brought Lazarus' family to the realization that only He, Jesus, was the resurrection and the life.

Where Do I Turn?

What do you do when there is nothing else to do? Gospel singer Dottie Rambo summed up the lessons I learned about the love of God in her song "I Go to the Rock." The Rock is where I turn and how I keep going. I just do not quit, because the Rock of Ages is my solid foundation.

For me, this is what love looks like. It is having the immoveable, unshakable God to run to, who will embrace you and hold you through anything the devil or just plain life has to throw at you. We are overcomers as the love of Christ breaks through even our temporary darkest moments!

Resting in His everlasting love,
Harry R. Jackson Jr.

Harry R. Jackson Jr. is senior pastor of Hope Christian Church, near the nation's capital, and presiding bishop of the International Communion of Evangelical Churches. He is also the founder and chairman of the High Impact Leadership Coalition. Information about his ministries is available at http://www.thehopeconnection.org.

9

The Love War

By Patricia King

By this all men will know that you are My disciples,
if you have love for one another.

John 13:35 NKJV

When I was in my early twenties, I was married and the mother of two young boys. Outwardly I appeared a happy, free-spirited woman. But within my own heart, I was chained in a prison of darkness, depression and hopelessness.

Why? I had made choices as a teenager and young adult that violated my conscience, so I was now laden with guilt and shame. I felt like a bad person, walking in lies to cover up the shame of my earlier choices. I was also filled with fear, especially the fear of rejection. If people knew how evil I was, I was convinced they would reject me and even expose me publicly. So I drowned myself daily in alcohol, and sometimes got stoned on marijuana, trying to find at least a small measure of peace and escape. But these substances betrayed me terribly and only added to my guilt and shame. No one—not even my husband, who was often away on business—knew what was going on behind our closed doors. But I knew my choices were hurting me and those whom I loved dearly.

Trying to get off the treadmill of self-condemnation, I took motivational courses and studied psychology in an evening college program. But every attempt to improve myself simply confirmed my hopelessness. I tried to get spiritual help through the New Age, a form of spirituality, but found no personal breakthrough, only more brokenness. I went to medical doctors to see if there were any physiological reasons for how bad I felt, but they found nothing wrong.

I was alone, then, with my battle, filled with self-hatred, fear, condemnation, rejection and shame. I was living a life of lies and addiction. It was the darkest season of my life.

I could not keep living like this. I needed to talk with someone, to bring some of the darkness out into the open. But if I did, I felt I could lose everything—including my children. I was convinced that I needed to be institutionalized to keep my children safe. But if I were committed, I might never see them again.

With no options left, at the end of my rope, I resolved to disclose my addiction to my husband. Since he was away so often, he was unaware of the layers of deception in my life. But before I did, I also decided to contact a priest and arrange to have my younger son christened, as his older brother had been before him. Perhaps this way, if I were institutionalized, I would see my children again one day in heaven.

Love, Peace and Hope

So it was that one Thursday afternoon in December, I looked up a local Anglican church in the yellow pages—since I had grown up attending an Anglican Sunday school—and called the priest.

I gave him my name. Then I said, "I'm in a crisis in my life, and I want you to christen my son this Sunday."

"That's not possible," he replied. "You and your husband will need to take some classes first so that you understand the commitment."

What? His response shocked me. Rage began to rise inside me. *How dare he deny me the right to have my own child christened?* And after another minute or so, I slammed the phone down.

Within twenty minutes my doorbell rang. Who should be standing there when I opened the door? That priest had written my name down and looked me up in the phone book!

With a phony smile to conceal my shock, and with just as phony a voice, I said, "Well, hello, how nice to see you. Please come in."

I served him some tea and we talked for a while. I tried to impress him with my spirituality by sharing stories about my spiritual encounters in the New Age. He showed no sign of surprise, neither approval nor disapproval. He simply listened quietly and let me do all the talking.

And did I ever talk! As I did, I saw peace and love in his eyes.

After I finished what I knew was an impressive discourse, he shared his own personal journey in coming to know Jesus. He had been a priest for seventeen years, he explained, but it had only been in the last two years that he had had a personal experience with Jesus.

That surprised me. "How could you be a priest," I asked, "and not know God?" I thought all priests knew God and could connect you to Him.

"There's a difference," he replied, "between being religious and knowing God."

That caught my attention. Then he explained how he and many members of his congregation had recently encountered what he called the born-again experience and had been filled with the Holy Spirit, with the evidence of a spiritual language called tongues—speaking a language they did not understand.

Once again something inside me began to go ballistic. I loved spiritual experiences and listening to my New Age friends share strange spiritual encounters. Yet here I was, reacting strongly to this kind priest sharing another strange spiritual encounter, a gift called tongues.

I tried to hide my agitation as I told myself, *This guy is totally nuts—get him out of your house.*

He was getting ready to leave. But before he did, he invited me to a Bible study the following Tuesday night. People in his church who were born again and speaking in tongues met to study the Bible and have what he called "fellowship."

Are you kidding? I thought. *I wouldn't be caught dead with those people.*

But I concealed my disgust, gave him another phony smile and said, "Thank you for the invitation. I'm not sure if I'm available."

I was glad when he left. I was not interested in seeing that tongues-talking priest again. And I was *not* showing up at his Bible study with his nutty congregation.

But from the time he left my home that Thursday afternoon until the following Tuesday, my insides twisted in torment. Part of me longed to go to the meeting because I was so hungry for freedom. I kept remembering the love in that priest's eyes and the peace he seemed to have. Maybe I could find hope with those people.

But something else within me, almost like a demon, resisted the idea violently. *I wouldn't be caught dead in that meeting,* I thought, *with all those off-balance people.*

The war raged for four days. Finally, on Tuesday afternoon, I decided to settle the issue. I marched over to the house of my Catholic neighbor to offer her an invitation I knew she would decline. She had informed me previously that, according to her parish rules, she was not permitted to attend the services of another denomination. It was my way out. Her saying no would settle my internal battle. At least I had given it a try.

"An *Anglican* priest came to my home," I said pointedly, "and invited me to an *Anglican* Bible study. They do really weird things like praying in spiritual languages they don't understand. I don't want to go, but I thought if you wanted to go with me, I would attend."

"Sure," she belted out in a hearty voice. "I'd love to go with you."

I was shocked. And now I was stuck.

The next few hours were torment. Something inside me kept squirming big-time. But I got a babysitter for the boys, met my neighbor and we drove a short distance to the Bible study. I was actually trembling physically.

But when the host opened the door, peace flooded me from the top of my head to the soles of my feet. All my fear was gone. Never had I felt peace like that!

The priest had prepared the attendees for my possible appearance. I could tell from what they said that they had been praying for me. Somehow I did not mind.

The meeting itself was interesting and lively. They sang songs with a songleader playing a guitar. As a child I had been accustomed to serious, melancholy services where you sang out of a hymnal as the organ played solemnly in the background. But these people were unusually happy. They sang with all their hearts and clapped their hands. I had never attended a happy church service, and was unfamiliar with the joy the people exuded. They were so full of light that their faces shone. I felt dark in comparison. When they sang in tongues, I loved it. It sounded like angels' voices. And they all shared testimonies about how Jesus had come into their hearts, forgiven them all their sins and past mistakes and given them brand-new lives.

Every story sparked hope within me. Listening to story after story, and thinking that I, too, might be able to begin again, and that perhaps God could forgive my sins, was almost too much to contain.

Love Lifted Me

Later, after I sent the babysitter home, I sat in my living room, thinking about the meeting. Around midnight, I knelt on the floor and began to weep uncontrollably. I longed to experience what the believers up the street had talked about. I felt evil but did not want to be evil. I wanted what they had, but I was trapped in a cell of shame and guilt, unworthy of love, unworthy even to live. Where did God draw the line? The sins they mentioned in their testimonies did not seem as evil as mine. Maybe He would not want the likes of me. I was desperate, yet desperately afraid of His rejection. What if I asked Him to help me and He said no?

The darkness of my sin weighed heavily on me, but I knew I had to take the risk. I did not know how to pray, and felt awkward as I stumbled to share my heart with this invisible God called Jesus.

"Jesus, I don't know how to talk to You," I said, "so I might not do this right. But I want You. Those people up the street said that You came into their lives and took their sin away and gave them brand-new lives. I would like that, too, Jesus. I would like You to come into my heart. I want You to be my God."

As I blurted out this prayer, tormenting thoughts came from deep inside: *What if He says no? What if He doesn't want you? Then what?*

But He did not hesitate even for a moment. I had not even finished praying my feeble prayer before I experienced what I can only describe as liquid love filling my entire body. I was filled with Jesus' life-transforming love. I could actually feel the weight of the relentless guilt and shame leave me. In one moment of time, Love Himself overcame the power of darkness in my life.

I wept and wept, kneeling on the living room floor, as the burden and oppression I had lived under for years left me. I knew that Jesus was aware of everything I had ever done behind closed doors. He was the only One who knew everything, absolutely everything, yet I also knew He loved me without conditions. He accepted me perfectly and completely. Love Himself had set me free.

There in the living room as the hours passed, I felt new within. I knew God had given me a brand-new life. I did not deserve it, yet He was lavishing me with mercy, love and forgiveness.

All night long I cried tears of gratitude as wave after wave of love continued to flood over me. I was completely wrecked by His love. There would be no turning back.

Finally, about six in the morning, I got up off the floor. Noticing that the lights were on directly across the walkway from our town house, and figures were moving around, I was filled with an urge to tell my neighbors what had just happened. They were apparently up and getting ready for work, and my boys were still asleep. So I hurried across the walkway and knocked on their door.

It was the husband who came to the door.

I gushed, "Last night Jesus came into my heart, took away all my sin and gave me a brand-new life. He can give you one, too, if you want."

He looked at me, speechless at first. Then, after what seemed like a long pause, he asked, "Patricia, have you gone crazy? What are you doing?"

"I was crazy," I replied joyfully, "but now I'm not crazy."

He looked disgusted, muttered something about getting ready for work and shut the door.

He and his wife were not my first converts. In fact, I think they helped spread the word that Patricia had gone "off her rocker" and become a religious fanatic. But love compelled me to go to them, wisely or unwisely, that morning. I was convinced that the only reason they and the whole world were not saved yet was simply because they had not heard. I was in love with Jesus and nothing else mattered.

I was soon to learn from my new reading of the Bible that when you are forgiven much, you love much. Jesus told the Pharisee concerning the sinful woman, "Her sins, which are many, are forgiven, for she loved much. But to whom little is forgiven, the same loves little" (Luke 7:47 NKJV).

That night in December, when I was born again by the love of God, my darkest hour gave birth to the brightest day in my life. Love had transformed me. And when you know you are loved, you are free.

I love this old hymn, "Love Lifted Me" (lyrics James Rowe, music Howard E. Smith):

> Love lifted me! Love lifted me!
> When nothing else could help, Love lifted me!

That is the song of my heart.

In the coming years, pastors, leaders and Christian friends mentored me beautifully in the love and grace of our Lord Jesus Christ. It was easy for me to forgive others and show mercy to those who were struggling, because I had received so much love, forgiveness and mercy myself. Carnal flesh is ugly—and at times we all manifest unredeemed flesh with its rotten choices and attitudes. Yet God is faithful when we err, and calls us back to Himself and His righteousness by love. He disciplines us in love, yet is patient, steadfast and unwavering in His adoring relationship with us.

This is how we should treat others, too. There is no room for self-righteousness in the Body of Christ. We were all shown mercy in our darkest hours, receiving His love freely when we least deserved it, and we can give it to others freely, even when it seems unwarranted.

Back to the Love War

Decades passed. I had my share of trials and dark moments as I discovered that as one's sphere of influence increases, so do one's trials and tests. God is always good, and anything that does not appear good is actually a gift that offers us a glorious "faith test" or "love test." Through the glorious tests I have faced—I mean "gifts," of course!—I have learned some valuable lessons. Each test helped bring me to the end of myself, enabling me to identify with the goal of the apostle Paul: "that I may know Him and the power of His resurrection, and the fellowship of His sufferings, being conformed to His death" (Philippians 3:10 NKJV).

Foremost of these tests was one that started the same year I had started teaching about the glory of God and the supernatural. I was with ministry colleagues who had been in the trenches of frontline battle together for years. We had sacrificed our lives, finances, time and gifts for the advancement of the Kingdom in my beloved nation of Canada. We trusted each other. We loved each other.

Late one night, a few of them were asking me probing questions regarding my teaching about the glory realm. I was happy and excited to answer their questions and share what I believed the Lord had given me on the subject during a thirty-day heavenly visitation a year earlier.

But my answers did not seem to satisfy them. Finally, after sustained discussion, one of them declared, "You are deceived, and you are deceiving the people."

I could hardly believe my ears.

"What do you mean?" I asked. "Where do you feel I'm deceived?"

"You're in rebellion."

I had never intentionally walked in rebellion in all the years I had known the Lord, either against Him or against my colleagues in ministry. But none of them, it seemed, supported me. I felt undone.

We parted that night in disagreement, which over the next few weeks became even more intense. Reports spread throughout Canada and into the United States about my "deception." A dear friend stepped down as my advisor and asked me not to be in touch anymore. Other friends emailed that because of the heat of the controversy over my life, they were withdrawing from relationship at this time.

Every day brought more problems. My heart felt like mincemeat. I was shredded within, crying day and night.

But I lay down my teaching and, over the next few months, pursued a process of spiritual discernment from people I respected. Since the nature of deception is that you cannot see you are in it, I wanted the truth and did not care how painful it would be. If I needed discipline, I would embrace it. If I was in error, I would admit it publicly and repent.

The results of these examinations encouraged me that I was not in rebellion. They also gave me welcome biblical counsel. But they did not terminate the assaults. I experienced alienation from many individuals and sectors in the Body of Christ. Negative reports had spread like wildfire. Respected leaders renounced my teachings. Petitions were written against me and sent to churches in entire regions.

Over the next months, and then years, some brothers and sisters reached out with love and kindness. They took the heat with me and for me. But I began to feel tired and beaten down. One morning about five years after the initial confrontation, I awakened feeling particularly down. I had read discouraging reports on the Internet the night before, and woke up wanting to "ascend" into heaven and maybe never "descend." I was not suicidal; I just wanted to leave the pressure and pain behind.

As I mentally reviewed some of the painful events of the last five years, I heard myself exclaim with a loud and commanding voice, "I declare war!"

Yikes! What had I just said? I knew for sure—like one hundred percent—that I did not want war. I wanted peace.

But as I tried to resist what I had heard come out of my own mouth, I heard another loud proclamation from deep within: "I declare war!"

Again I struggled against it. Yet a third time I heard my own command: "I declare war! A love war!"

In that moment I experienced a surge of enlightenment and the awareness of a tool that would secure ultimate victory: *love.*

I had found my place to stand. Love would be my greatest weapon against discouragement and oppression. I would try to be like Jesus and walk as He walked. Jesus never withdrew love, and He never lost faith when He lived His life on earth, no matter what He faced. He always loved.

And on this special morning, I knew I was being offered the opportunity of a lifetime. Jesus was inviting me to know "the fellowship of His sufferings" in a way I had never known before. I was being invited to be like Him and to embrace the cross of His unconditional love.

Winning the War with Love

What does that mean? How do we embrace the cross?

Through Jesus' journey to the cross, and through the pain He endured for us, He passed every love test and every faith test. He was betrayed by a close disciple and denied by one of His dearest friends. The Bible says He was abandoned by all His disciples in His darkest hour: "They all forsook him and fled" (Mark 14:50 NKJV). The perfect Lamb of God was slandered, beaten, lied about, scourged, humiliated and crucified, yet He never lost faith and He never withdrew His love.

We are sinners just like those who treated Him cruelly. Our carnal flesh, like theirs, was at enmity with Him before we were made new through salvation: "All have sinned and fall short of the glory of God" (Romans 3:23 NKJV). But Jesus Christ died to Himself in every respect so that we might live. God "made Him who knew no sin to be sin for us, that we might become the righteousness of God in Him" (2 Corinthians 5:21 NKJV). So it was that the apostle John exclaimed, "Behold what manner of love the Father has bestowed on us, that we should be called children of God!" (1 John 3:1 NKJV).

Only love can produce pure humility. Jesus humbled Himself through His love for us, and as a result, He became the greatest in the Kingdom:

> He humbled Himself and became obedient to the point of death, even the death of the cross. Therefore God also has highly exalted Him and given Him the name which is above every name, that at the name of Jesus every knee should bow, of those in heaven, and of those on earth, and of those under the earth, and that every tongue should confess that Jesus Christ is Lord, to the glory of God the Father.
>
> Philippians 2:8–11 NKJV

Jesus Christ is the King of love! The battle for mankind's salvation was won by love. None of us deserved it, but love won the war for our souls.

And the unfailing sacrifice of giving oneself for others is what true love looks like. Such love never fails. It is that love that gives us the power to overcome in our darkest hour.

Jesus said, "In the world, you will have tribulation" (John 16:33 NKJV). That is a promise! Everyone faces hardship, betrayal and temptation. But how a person handles them determines the outcome. Your tests and trials can be stumbling blocks or stepping-stones, depending on your perspective and the choices you make under pressure. The sufferings of Jesus were love sufferings. And every trial we go through can lead us to a greater understanding of His love.

You will never know how much real love you have in you until you face opposition or even persecution. It is easy to say, "I love you," but you will not actually know if that confession is true until that love is tested. Many couples say they love each other, but few in our times pass the test of covenant love following marriage.

Do we fully understand the price of love? Do we understand that every love test will give us the opportunity to love like Jesus? When your love is put to the test, you will find out how much real love is actually operating in your life.

If love is our greatest weapon, then how should we respond when we are mistreated or even slandered?

Enlisting in the Love War

On that memorable morning, the Lord reminded me that His love had not only lifted me, saved me and delivered me in my darkest hour, decades earlier, but also that it would not fail me now, in the midst of this dark season. He invited me to know the fellowship of His sufferings and to embrace the cross of His love.

Was I willing to win the war with love and more love?

Was I willing to explore the depths of His love and embrace my own cross of suffering in order to know the fellowship of His sufferings?

Was I willing to make love my greatest aim and believe in its power to protect, reconcile and bless?

I said *yes* that morning to the love war. Love was not a negotiable. I had no plan B. Love would win the war.

Over the following months and years, with ongoing winds of tribulation, I witnessed the power of God's love at work. What a glorious journey of discovery! I learned much about the cross and how to die to my own pain and needs in order to better serve and love others. I learned to embrace the fellowship of His sufferings by honoring when I felt dishonored, showing mercy when I was criticized, covering others when I was wrongfully exposed, forgiving others when I felt mistreated and misunderstood, and accepting when I was rejected.

We all make mistakes. We all have failed in love. It is important to remember that about ourselves when others fail us. We all are in this boat of humanity together. We all are love failures without Christ's intervention. I could write an entire book on my love failures. Remembering my failures makes it easy for me to show grace and honor to others when they fail in loving me.

I also experienced the extravagant rewards of love in that season. Favor and anointing began to increase. Fruitful ministry resulted. Financial blessings increased. And I came to peace with those who had resisted me. In fact, these became some of my dearest and most treasured relationships. I watched God restore friendships, ministry alliances and trust.

Jesus said, "By this all will know that you are My disciples, if you have love for one another" (John 13:35 NKJV).

The Church is known for many things. Unfortunately we are not known for our love. One day we will all stand before God, and as the prophet Bob Jones shared about a heavenly visitation (Stacey Campbell tells the story in chapter 1 of this book), the Lord will ask everyone the same question: "Did you learn how to love?"

Without love, as the apostle Paul teaches in 1 Corinthians 13, we are nothing, we have nothing and we are profited nothing. Love is the principal thing, and while we live on the earth, we are in a war—the love war.

In my darkest hours, love has lifted and transformed me. In the darkness of the world around us, love will once again lift and transform. The vilest sinner will be transformed, unity and peace will fill the Body of Christ, enemies will be reconciled and entire nations will be visited by love.

Enlist today in the love war!

Patricia King

Patricia King is a television host, media producer, co-founder of XPmedia .com and apostolic founder and leader of XPministries. She hosts the Everlasting Love TV program. Information about her ministries is available at http://www.patriciaking.com.

10

Love Is a Revelation

By Mickey Robinson

Therefore if anyone is in Christ, he is a new creature; the old things passed away; behold, new things
have come.

2 Corinthians 5:17 NASB

As a storyteller, I could easily slip into a really lyrical
mode in describing the topic of this book, what love
looks like. Love—searching for it, finding it, losing it or
never having known it—may be the common denominator of
all human drama. In the world love is temporal, and possibly
for some in an extended way, generational. Even the highest
form of human love, however, cannot compare to the love of
God. The love of God is seminal. It is the origin and the creative force of *real love*.

So much for a discourse on the theory of what love looks like; I want to keep it real by talking about love in my personal experiences. Love is authentic, raw and magnificent. And for me, love is a revelation.

Perhaps the best way to describe what love looks like is by contrasting it with darkness. A blind person would have no concept of vision until he or she could see for the first time. In my opinion, most people do not know what darkness is until they see light. That would be me when it comes to love.

Young and Restless

I was born into the Baby Boomer generation in the last half of the twentieth century. In our nation and culture, we were remiss in our understanding of economic hardship and political oppression. Ours was the opposite—a golden era of America filled with freedom, prosperity and unlimited promise. The good guys were good, and the bad guys were bad. My childhood hero, Superman, would always defeat the bad guys and then humbly disguise himself as Clark Kent, a regular American middle-class man. The American dream was not just to be better; it was to be the best! Winners got the honor, the money and, of course, the pretty girl, and they lived happily ever after.

In the arena of human endeavor, achievement equaled attainment. I skated through grade school, involved with team sports and groups of friends who stuck together like clans. I devotedly studied all aspects of aviation. From the Wright brothers to NASA, I memorized it all. Somehow, I wanted to become part of the adventure of flying. This ambition permeated my life as I moved from parochial church school into public high school. I acquired an appetite to fill my life with excitement, adventure and pleasure. Sports was one example. It was not about playing; it was about playing to win. Winning was about getting the rewards—"to the victor go the spoils."

Extremely gifted in sports, I found favor in the clique of gifted athletes. At an early age, I worked and saved money so I could buy my own stuff—the right clothes, my own car and ski equipment. I grew up in the suburbs of Cleveland, Ohio, the birthplace of rock 'n' roll. Socially, I became part of the "in crowd," attending dances and being invited to the best parties.

Four days after I graduated from high school, on my eighteenth birthday, I began working in a prestigious stock brokerage firm. After just a few months, I was promoted. I was trading stock at lightning speed and being groomed into the brave new world of progressive finance—heady wine for a young and restless soul who always wanted more.

Never Saw It Coming

Nine months later, I jumped out of an airplane for the first time. That instant connected me to a source of pleasure I had dreamed about as a child. I literally felt as if I could fly. My enthusiasm and athletic skill propelled me into this new realm of gratification called free fall. So all-consuming was my commitment that I allocated all my time to planning my next jump. I literally lived for that moment. With every jump, my hunger for it grew.

I never saw it coming. One hot summer night in mid-August, I boarded a plane with four other skydivers and a pilot. We took off for a routine practice jump and suddenly had total engine failure. We plunged to the earth with deadly velocity. The plane slammed into a tree, and then careened over and wedged into the earth. The last skydiver escaped the plane just before it exploded into flames.

On impact, my head had rammed into the instrument panel. Though not unconscious, I was completely out of it, yet still trying to escape. Soaked with fuel, I was on fire from head to toe. My skydiving partner fearlessly ran back into the death trap and pulled me free. With strenuous effort, the fire was extinguished. Once paramedics loaded me into an ambulance, they raced to the nearest hospital.

Then that self-sufficient young man I had become called out to a God I did not know and had never served: "Help me! I'm sorry! I want another chance!"

My injuries were totally catastrophic. Massive third-degree burns, head trauma, lacerations and blindness in my right eye. The medical team determined that I would die of shock before the first night was over.

I did survive that night, and they went to battle for me with all that science and medicine had to offer. In a short period of time, however, my complications became overwhelming. My finely tuned body rapidly deteriorated, with massive weight loss and deadly infections that spread all over my body and throughout my circulatory system. At times I was bleeding ten pints of blood a day. After consulting an expert from a world-famous hospital, the medical staff determined there was no hope for me.

From that point on, the ministers of medicine gave up trying to save my life, and I entered into "the valley of the shadow of death" (see Psalm 23). A few weeks before this incident, I was oblivious to thoughts of death, right or wrong and the afterlife. I also was oblivious to the importance of knowing God. Blinded by my ambition and feeling as though I had my act together, I was living from one breath to another.

The day the doctor told my family I would die, a strange and eerie feeling crept over me. My whole system began shutting down. As my body rattled in throbbing pain, I became super-conscious and felt my spirit thrust out of my physical body. I was gliding through another dimension, a spiritual world.

Instantaneously, multiple revelations of understanding stunned me. I realized, *I am a spirit, and I have a soul.* And the most shocking discovery of all: *There is an eternity! Forever is forever!*

The Revelation of Eternity

Chronological time is connected to the physical plane of created things. Everything spiritual is continual and everlasting. I was experiencing my first revelation of eternity. Its rich colors astonished me, as did the freedom I felt at being out of the physical dimension. Without any control on my part, I was gliding toward the purest white light, a portal of entrance that emanated a *compelling peace.*

Feeling pressure on my right side, I turned and looked. What I saw was a black abyss—an eternal, bottomless pit. I could feel the nature of it: everlasting solitary confinement, nonnegotiable separation from the source of all life. My spirit man had glided to the entrance of the white portal, but I was now being eclipsed, almost as if I were being swallowed by this outer darkness.

I cried out the same desperate plea: "I'm sorry! Help me, please! I want to live!"

Thrust through this white portal, I burst into God's presence, in the third heaven. Instantly I knew I would never die, forever and ever. The majesty and glory of God were everywhere. Somewhere to my immediate left, I sensed the very presence of God Himself. I was standing in the glory of what is called the River of Life.

The ecstasy I felt is impossible to describe. The single most stunning aspect of this heavenly encounter was the pure and personal love of this Holy God for me. Love is a revelation, and I knew from that moment that it is everlasting.

The Father's love extracted me out of the absolute depths of final darkness and conveyed me into the Kingdom of the Son of His love (see Colossians 1:13). I experienced many revelations in this heavenly encounter, all governed by Supreme Love. Then I was sent back. As my spirit man reentered my battered body, I woke up in perfect peace that surpassed all understanding (see Philippians 4:7). Darkness flees from the light of His perfect love.

His Love Makes All Things New

What does breakthrough love look like? Majestic power and beauty that makes *all things new*. I was blind, and now I see the love that is a revelation of Jesus Christ, my Lord, Messiah and Healer. Love is a revelation that never fails and never ends.

Seeing what love looks like involves our perception. We need to see how the love of God brings about change. My life's journey could be seen as a three-act play in which the love of God kept changing me (and still does). Act I was from birth to the time of my personal collision with human mortality. Then love rushed upon me with the redeeming power of a revelation of God's forgiveness and acceptance.

To know what love looks like, one must be able to recognize it and see it as it really is. I believe that takes the spirit of wisdom and revelation. As we come to know and understand the very nature of God, our new nature also is revealed. In the gospel of John the beloved, John uses the contrast between light and darkness to declare the nature, purpose and preeminence of our Lord:

> And the light shines in the darkness, and the darkness did not *comprehend* it.

There was a man sent from God, whose name was John. This man came for a witness, to bear witness of the Light, that all through him might believe. He was not that Light, but was sent to bear witness of that Light. That was the true Light which gives light to every man coming into the world.

John 1:5–9 NKJV, emphasis added

A skeptic might say, "If God is everywhere, why is He so hard to find?" The Greek word used in this passage for *comprehend* means to lay hold of, to perceive, or in other words, *to see* by revelation. The darkness does not get it and is unreceptive to it. The ecstatic joy for a true believer should be a thankful appreciation that once you get it, you've got it!

Following my revelation, I was comforted before there was any manifestation of change in my physical body. For me, that was one of the most amazing aspects of the colossal power of what God's love looks like. How could someone who was in every way completely uncomfortable be comforted? In receiving the love of God, I was so flooded with it that I loved everything and everybody. Even though I had all sorts of deadly medical complications and no hope in natural terms, I was ecstatic and enraptured in Super Love.

Light, then, is a superior authority and a force far above all darkness. All the king's horses and all the king's men could not put Mickey back together again, so to speak. But God, who is rich in mercy, began a continual healing process that can only be described as supernatural. I give a detailed account of that story in my book *Falling into Heaven: A Skydiver's Gripping Account of Heaven, Healings, and Miracles* (Broadstreet, 2014).

In addition to being a revelation, one of the things love looks like is *restoration*. I literally had suffered the loss of all things, but I gained the knowledge and revelation of who God really is. Numerous miracles, healings and supernatural encounters all produced restorative results. The medical people said I would never walk again. I have since jumped out of airplanes. I am also a snow skier, and I still play American football on Thanksgiving. Blind in my right eye for five and half years, I had my eyesight restored, to the amazement of the elite eye surgeons who saw under a microscope that my eye was dead. The list of the physical mountains of healing I have climbed goes on and on. Yet the greatest evidence of what breakthrough love looks like comes in the revelation of God's personal love for me individually, and for each one of us.

Closing the Curtain on Act I

All of my life leading up to my accident, relationships had been meaningful— even critical—to my well-being. Though outwardly I may have looked like a confident, cheerful and charismatic young man, I lived in what we would now call a dysfunctional family. My father was a hard worker, but he was also an alcoholic with an explosive temper. And for some reason unknown to me, he always picked on me and never told me he loved me. He never complimented me, but rather mocked and ridiculed me in my attempts to find meaningful purpose for my life. I kept these hurts to myself, buried deep in denial. I was unaware then of how destructive a "father wound" can be when left to fester into an emotional infection.

Since my family relationships were painfully damaged, I sought social relationships with my peers. The most significant, of course, was a serious romantic relationship. After the crash, the girl of my dreams represented the only attachment I felt I had left to life as I had known it before the crash. I planned to propose to her at Christmas, but in the spring of 1969, I received a painful phone call from her. She said our life together was over.

I was devastated. I was just getting a little better and beginning to think I would survive, and then the emotional bottom fell out. The result was a feeling that I had truly lost everything in the crash.

I now understand that I expected the love of a person to fill a place that is only filled by receiving the love of God the Father, Son and Holy Spirit. The process of the power of God binding up my broken heart took place deep inside, while I was being healed and restored. I know now that unless you mourn, you cannot be comforted.

"Hope deferred makes the heart sick, but desire fulfilled is a tree of life" (Proverbs 13:12 NASB). This is not a riddle, but a severe reality that I both suffered from and found relief from. It took godly wisdom to be able to love again. My relationship with the girl of my dreams technically died at the crash site. My emotions were still attached, however. Possibly they fell into the category of a "soul tie," something I had never heard of at the time. I could feel the intensity of them, unrealistic though they were, which is the case with soul ties. A person's feelings are real in a soul tie, but are not realistic.

Contrary to the popular saying, time does *not* heal all wounds—unless you allow the Healer into that inner chamber to take care of the wound. Like Lazarus, I was raised from the dead but still wrapped in grave clothes. I did find some emotional resolution when I attended a close friend's wedding and faced my high school clan and my former girlfriend. As I walked out of that church, I saw that I had totally disconnected from everybody I had once been close to and everything I had once been. I realized that the old Mickey Robinson was dead, and I was consciously becoming aware of the man who had taken his place. It was obvious on a conscious level, anyway, and I made mental assent to it by acknowledging the final loss of those relationships. I buried my emotions, however—buried them alive!

When I got back into the rehab hospital, I focused on restoring my health. I embraced the painful therapy like a challenging game. The healings accelerated, and the medical team said everything went beyond their expectations. Also, inexplicable healings and miracles took place, such as an instant return of the use of my legs after they were diagnosed as having permanently damaged nerves.

During this process my passion was for complete restoration of my life. I had no one to talk to, though, about my spiritual encounters and what these things meant.

For the next five years, I was constantly admitted to the hospital for reconstructive and plastic surgery. When I was home recovering, I was on a personal quest to find the meaning of life. The revolutionary upheaval of the late 1960s and early '70s opened doors to all manner of spiritual beliefs and lifestyle adventures. Through music, the rock artists preached permission to experiment with free love, recreational drugs and various spiritual beliefs and no boundaries. I was full of love and experienced supernatural peace, yet naïve enough to love everybody and not be discerning about certain things. As the years of my healing went on, I kept engaging in trying to find true spirituality and my purpose in life.

Then Love Came—For a While

Act II of my life started when I met beautiful Barbara, who is now my wife, in February 1973. Ours was a whirlwind relationship that was unorthodox and highly idealistic. She stood up to accept the Lord at a rock concert one month after we met. She loved me even in my half-charred condition. We purchased an old farmhouse and a barn with some acreage and began our life together in December of that year. Through our early years, we started meeting some Christians from the Jesus People movement, but we never really got established in any type of ongoing fellowship. I was trying to build an ideal/

utopian life in this world and find an external peace that just kept escaping me.

It all came to a head in February 1975. My life got stripped down to nothing, again. Even Barbara fell into a web of delusion and left me. I was totally alone. The Lord was really dealing with me about laying down everything, absolutely everything, and completely trusting Him. He challenged me to follow Him into unknown territory.

While deep in prayer and fasting, I faced a frontal assault from the enemy. Through crafty spiritual warfare, a *voice of darkness* wove together all the events of my life and made it appear that I had caused all my own problems. It so oppressed me that I sat alongside a creek bed at our farm property, almost paralyzed by the threatening lies. Diabolically, the assault lasted for several hours. I endured through the pain, loneliness and anguish of it, while not letting go of the Lord, who had not let go of me.

Then spontaneously, the voice of the Holy Spirit came from behind me and went through me, saying, *What you did was an act of love.*

Those eight words from the Holy Spirit were like a nuclear bomb blowing up all the structure and strategy being orchestrated by my enemy, the accuser of the brethren (see Revelation 12:9–10).

I got up, went into our farmhouse and freely prayed, "Father, I don't understand all of this. It doesn't make sense. But please, I release everything to You. Protect Barbara from any hurt. I'll follow You anywhere—no matter what!"

The Lord was asking me to be willing to give up everything, even Barbara, and embrace my life with Him. At the same time I was doing that, the Holy Spirit fell on Barbara four hundred miles away. She was gloriously filled with power and wrote out a prophecy about her dedication to the Lord and her commitment to me. We were reunited immediately.

I had been severely challenged, but love broke through. In this instance, love looked like "a mighty warrior" as what the enemy had meant for evil God turned for good. Jeremiah 20:11 (NASB) says, "But the LORD is with me like a dread champion; therefore my persecutors will stumble and not prevail."

Amazingly, Barbara and I found some radical Christians right in the area where we lived. Then everything began to fall into place as we put it all into God's hands.

Closing the Curtain on Act II

Barbara and I found such joy being in fellowship, worshiping, having people to pray with and growing every day in the Lord. We soon found the community of believers was everywhere. The raw excitement of the Jesus movement was contagious. People were not just enthusiastic; they were passionately on fire and unstoppable in sharing their faith with everyone. No one was off-limits or unapproachable. It was common for people to share their personal testimonies in radical house meetings, which were a normal part of these vibrant new local churches that were springing up.

Very soon I was asked to share my testimony in a variety of different places. I would devour Scripture, constantly play the latest contemporary Christian music, and never miss a meeting anywhere the grace of God was being poured out. Surprisingly, I had quite an aptitude for the Bible, and the spiritual gifts were increasing in me all the time. Yet I was not quite ready for the surprise when Barbara told me we were having a baby! Michael Robinson was born on March 4, 1975. Barbara had a little difficulty in the last two months of the pregnancy, and Michael was five weeks premature. But everything about him seemed beautiful, and we basked in the mystery and beauty of being first-time parents.

Three or four months after Michael was born, the doctor observed that he was not developing orthopedically in some areas. Being an observant mother, Barbara had actually noticed it before the doctor said anything. Michael was not holding his head up quite as strongly as some of the infants in the nursery, and he did not begin crawling around as soon.

It was not until Michael was a little over a year old that he was diagnosed with cerebral palsy. In every other way he was healthy; he spoke at an early age and was tender and affectionate. Upon hearing about his condition, we began fervent prayer for his healing. Strangely, we did not feel afraid, but had such joy in the Lord that we just took it in stride. We were surrounded by loving believers who joined us in prayer for Michael's specific need for healing. Our expectations were always high.

Taking the Leap Once Again

At about this time, the Lord saw fit to draft me into full-time ministry. This is when Act III of the love revelation in my life started. I had never thought about full-time ministry before and certainly did not volunteer for it. I began around the time our second son, Matthew, was born (March 26, 1978). Michael still was not walking, but we kept hoping.

Ministry opportunities grew, and I spoke in various places. We found a church in our hometown and became active in every area available to us. We met some folks there who had been in a rock band, and since I was a guitar player, we joined together and revolutionized the worship. Our worship band turned into an outreach band, and we played all kinds of places—churches, youth gatherings and hard-core prisons. We even played in the prison where the movie *The Shawshank Redemption* was filmed. We led hundreds and then thousands to the Lord in these various meetings.

We continued to pray for Michael's healing. When he grew too big for his large, handicap-oriented stroller, we reluctantly had him fitted for a wheelchair. Emotionally that was a hard decision. We wanted him healed and walking, and it felt as if we were giving in to something to order that wheelchair. But it was for his safety, so we yielded.

I was appointed the primary leader in our local church, and we found it exciting and rewarding to serve the Lord in those days of wonder. Barbara was a completely devoted, unselfishly dedicated, nurturing mother all through our ministry. When Michael was five, our third son, Jacob, was born at home in our farmhouse. Fifteen months later, Barbara was pregnant again.

When Barbara was four months along, Michael prophetically announced, "The baby's name is Elizabeth!"

No ultrasound was done, yet he was right. Elizabeth was born April 28, 1983. We regularly packed four kids into the family station wagon, along with a wheelchair, and never missed a single meeting. We also continued to pray for Michael's healing.

The Lord sent us to another church in a neighboring community, and our ministry grew again. I was ordained into a lead role there, and our ministry increased way beyond our local church. Meanwhile, we kept believing for Michael's healing.

The wife of one of the elders in our church once questioned me, "How can you go out and teach about healing while your son is in a wheelchair?"

Barbara and I were not offended. We knew people just did not get it. None of our peers or even our close friends knew what it was like to have a special-needs child. Actually, we did not know ourselves how much this was affecting our family. We just lived as if everything were "normal." That was part of what love looked like for us.

Once in his early teenage years, I heard *a sinister dark voice* say, *Michael will never have any friends*. It was unrelated to anything that was taking place at the time; it was simply "a sword to pierce my heart." In reality, he is perhaps the friendliest member of our family.

Facing More Trauma

A few years later, Michael required surgery to correct severe curvature of the spine. After a massive prayer covering and three consultations with three doctors, Michael underwent this radical surgical procedure. His back was cut open from the top of his neck past the base of his spine, and the doctors inserted metal rods, screws and wires.

When Barbara and I went in to see Michael afterward, he simply looked at me and said, "Dad, hold me."

He was so brave and yet in so much pain. I felt powerless to comfort him. In the weeks that followed, we never slept more than one hour at night as we tried to help him. During the operation certain nerves had been damaged, and he lost control of his bladder and bowel functions, which previously had been normal. As a result, his personal care became nearly impossible. One year after the surgery, we laid down our church, sold our home and moved to East Texas at the invitation of a well-known ministry. We based our decision partly on our desire to seek further therapeutic help for our son.

The best rehab specialist in Dallas, Texas, did an assessment on Michael. When he released him, this specialist told us, "He will just keep getting worse and will have to spend the rest of his life in bed."

I thought I already knew all about desperation, but this felt like futility—a bad situation that kept getting worse and worse. We just kept going, however, as our ministry was reconfigured. I traveled and hosted conferences. We kept pressing on, even as Michael continued to face more trauma, and all of us along with him.

At one point, Michael suffered a grand mal seizure while we were away. I was shattered. *I can't even go away without unbearable trouble following me*, I thought. I was known as a great encourager, yet now I was despondent. At the time, we had been invited to go by boat out to an island with our friends and have dinner. I sat in the back of the boat and just stared, processing everything. Through our years together, Barbara had learned my ways. She knew if I was not talking, I needed to be left alone. As the big boat glided over the pristine water, I started having visions. I was seeing myself before large crowds in all kinds of places, including foreign countries. Great joy, healing and encouragement were showing all over this vast multitude of faces.

When the boat reached shore and my foot touched down on the wooden dock, I could not wait to get back home to go out and preach! There was not one hint of any good thing in view to resolve the dilemma of our pain and Michael's suffering, yet I was seeing what I would go out and do in God's power. Love broke through our unbearable pain through a revelation of what God had called me to do. I knew that He would care for my son, who is also His son.

Through an unexpected turn of events, Michael was admitted into a rehab hospital. A physical therapist there devoted himself to working with our son. All of Michael's previous abilities were restored except the nerve-damaged functions. That was fantastic news!

All the same, after Michael's failed operation my feelings were highly toxic. Strong emotions rose up in me that I had not experienced since becoming a Christian. I got angry at the hospital and doctors, some of whom had not been straightforward with us. I felt like a victim and blamed everybody. Yet I was still anointed and still moved in the power of the Holy Spirit to minister. Like Jeremiah, however, I felt like asking,

"Why has my pain been perpetual and my wound incurable, refusing to be healed?" (Jeremiah 15:18).

We were invited to move to Nashville, Tennessee, and we successfully found independent living for Michael. The care proved insufficient, however, so a few years ago we brought Michael back into our home. Barbara and I dropped all our other ministry to take care of him 24 hours a day, 7 days a week.

It was an authentic intervention for Michael, and as it turned out, it was also *secretly an intervention for me*. In some of the spiritual testing I have faced since Michael's dreadful operation, I have gotten more in touch with my inability to solve every problem or control everything. Today I know more than ever that I need God's love, God's help and God's strength.

Michael is still in that chair, but he is alive in faith. He prays. He prophesies. He even went to Mozambique to minister alongside his brother Matthew to release the relentless love of God.

God is faithful even when we are not. I am not the same man I once was. Love keeps breaking through and invading my life. Today, I have become a better husband, a loving father and a more Christlike guy. Our beautiful son Michael has steadily made progress, and we are yet passionately contending for his full and miraculous healing.

What Does Love Really Look Like?

Love looks like . . . a purifying fire. John the Baptist said, "One is coming who is mightier than I. . . . He will baptize you with the Holy Spirit and fire" (Luke 3:16 NASB). It is a fire of Holy Love—not that we would stand around it and be warmed, but that we would stand in it and be consumed!

Love looks like . . . commitment. God is committed to sanctify us by the fire of His love, so we might stand and not fall.

Love is not cheap; it is very costly. The crazy love of God is actually the most valuable commodity in this life. I know. I have been a grateful receiver of His amazing love, and I have set the course of my life to spread this revelation of the love of God one on one and around the world. His love is extravagant! His love is governmental.

Love *is* a revelation, an unfolding panorama of the nature, character and power of the One called Faithful and True. His love is unrelenting; it transforms us as we have our hope fixed on Him, Jesus. I love His love. I need His love. I trust you will abound all the more in His unfailing love.

Above all, put on love,
Mickey Robinson

Mickey and Barbara Robinson are co-founders of Prophetic Destiny International, a ministry that specializes in teaching, training and empowering people to live out their destinies. Information about his ministry is available at http://mickeyrobinson.com.

11

Light and Momentary Afflictions

By Jackie Pullinger

For our light affliction, which is but for a moment,
is working for us a far more exceeding and eternal
weight of glory.

2 Corinthians 4:17 NASB

have never been raped.
I have never been seriously abused.
I have never been lashed or stoned.
I have never been kidnapped or shipwrecked.
I have never been falsely imprisoned or brought to court.
I was never tricked or sold into slavery.

Indeed, must you inquire about my sufferings? The good times and the joy of Jesus so surely outweigh them that I can hardly remember them, let alone recount them for you. As it is said, "A woman, when she is in labor, has sorrow because her hour has come; but as soon as she has given birth to the child, she no longer remembers the anguish, for joy that a human being has been born into the world" (John 16:21 NKJV).

Here is Jackie, a twin born in wartime England within a fairly functional family. We had a house, a garden, we went to school, we had rationed food and games to play at mealtimes. I had shoes. I was loved and safe. We welcomed relations often, and the baker, the gardener, the milkman, the coal man were part of our lives. I had a little pocket money and passed-down clothes. And, without a sense of great need, I always had a sense of eternity and a sense that I was accountable to God for my life, my gifts and my sins.

One Day . . .

How could I imagine, though, what God had in store for me in the days to come? I had read about murderers.

"Did any repent and find Jesus before they were executed?" I asked my mother.

This was actually long before I knew Jesus' love for myself, but I felt it was important. I read about the hungry and the homeless. With my twin, I played about being in poor wood huts with no toilets. How could I know at that age of seven or eight that I was already one of the most wealthy and privileged people in the world? And I still am. In a world of hunger, slavery, abuse, lack of water and prejudice toward women, I am part of that unseen percentage that has been spared . . . all of that. "The lines have fallen to me in pleasant places; yes, I have a good inheritance" (Psalm 16:6 NKJV).

Let Me Take You on My Journey

I was not expecting suffering—though prepared for hardship. I only had one thing in mind. Having come to know the Lord in surprise and joy after studying at the Royal College of Music, I began to pray, as I had supposed as a child, that I would be ready to face Jesus when I died.

"Well done, you good and faithful servant."

These were the words I hardly dared to hope for. And having grown slowly and increasingly amazed at Jesus' love and sacrifice for me, it seemed there was only one way to spend my life. I expected not results—only the hope that as I had extraordinarily known His love, so He might use me to make Him known. However that might be. Wherever that might be.

So, I began a search. Where to go? Where to spend my life?

In God's mercy—as you might well know—I was refused by the only missionary agency I applied to. I also applied to other countries and organizations.

Well, the result was negative, but the call of God remained clear: "You must go."

It was an Abraham call. "By faith Abraham obeyed when he was called to go out to the place which he would receive as an inheritance. And he went out, not knowing where he was going" (Hebrews 11:8 NKJV).

My darling friend, a London vicar, encouraged me to get on a boat and see where I would land up. Maybe go all around the world just to talk to one sailor about Jesus. Maybe land up in Singapore to play the piano for a week of youth meetings. Maybe a shipwreck. *How wonderful,* I thought. It could be that there was one man on the island just waiting to know Jesus. How could I lose? With bells ringing in my heart and ten pounds in my pocket, I knew that I could trust God with my journey and my future. I had no expectations that I should achieve anything at all—just God's purpose.

I got on a ship. I landed in Hong Kong two months later. I was amazed that, with so little money, I could have free tea and coffee at the "church" I visited. What about the rest of the population who had nothing—and some who had nowhere to lay their heads at night? So, while experiencing God's provision for me, I ached for the street sleepers, the uncared-for grannies and those denied school. It seemed unfair. I had had every opportunity—even to make mistakes, but I had not lost my life because of them. Someone paid for my tram fare once. I was incredibly moved. Tea, coffee, cookies and a ten-cent tram ride. When would it be my turn to give?

In the midst of 1960s Hong Kong, there was so much need. Homelessness, refugees, hunger and a lack of welfare. No free education then, and crowded bed spaces. Families crammed into cocklofts. Children looking after babies, and the elderly begging. Where in all of Hong Kong should I be?

The City with Foundations

God led me to the Walled City—a wonderful place, though I had no idea what it was when I went there. From sixty thousand to eighty thousand people in five or six acres that made up a hidden city within Kowloon City. There was no law there. It was a political and historical fact that the police had no jurisdiction, though I later learned that they actually colluded in running the slave trade and were paid huge bribes by the gangsters who owned the drug dens.

There were no toilets, but open sewers beneath your feet, then tangled hanging wires of stolen electricity at head level and clanging plastics factories. Water was fetched through the stand pipes outside or the suspicious well within. Soon, I saw prostitutes or the old women who guarded them. At that time I knew not of the Triad gangs who controlled the drug and sex industries, but

I saw the crazy parodies of men who riffled through the sewers for hope of gain. It was known as the city of darkness. Heroin dens in tin tents where addicts "chased the dragon." Over forty stinking opium dens, but no sweetness nor glimpse of light.

I was not lonely. I did not miss my home or the country I had left. Why should I? God had made no mistake in sending one He knew could walk alone—after all, He formed me.

I can remember briefly crying for myself when arriving by mistake in Hung Hom, a district of Kowloon, when finding no one who spoke English to show me the way out. Which bus? I did cry, though, for the Walled City girls who were clearly imprisoned in stone cubicles, for the men whose bodies were dumped by the single toilet skirting the dark city, which had lured them with pipe dreams and poisoned them with drugs. Before they died, they were clearly visible lying in the squatter area just outside the Walled City border. There they straddled the lanes in dirty lines full of squalor and excrement, waiting for the awful time when they woke in pain and anguish. Then they were driven to steal, lie and cheat to get the next hit.

Two clear memories of the early days in Walled City, though I lived outside and supported myself by teaching in two excellent and prestigious schools. Firstly, I told God it would be worth my whole life to save just one of the wrecks I saw before they died. I asked Him to do it, adding that I did not mind knowing which wreck. I meant that. Secondly, I was aware of another city. I could see it. It was full of light. Streets for old men to sit in and children playing. Old women with needle marks on the backs of their hands started a new life when Jesus joined them on their wooden boxes. Their hands were healed and they no longer needed to spend their days "watching" the slave girls who funded their mean existence. Slimy, grimy men who were the watchmen of the gambling dens lifted their heads and smiled. And the mother who was beaten by her son for her whole day's labor separating plastics into sacks—she got a new son who had life in his veins instead of junk.

Of course I was seeing the City of God, the Kingdom of God, though I was not biblically familiar with the phrase at that time.

Abraham waited for the city that had foundations whose builder and maker is God. I desired a better country, a heavenly one. God is not ashamed to be called my God, for He has prepared a city for me (see Hebrews 11:8, 16).

The Price and the Prize

I have painted these pictures not to excite your admiration. Just be amazed that God chose me to be in such a place. I was not brave. I loved it and wondered why anyone on earth would want to be anywhere else. I was happy to be there for the rest of my life—I really was. It is probably called grace.

There followed years of meeting gangsters and loving their families. Blood and gang fights. I shared my apartment with street boys and briefly housed a girl we rescued from her boyfriend, who forcefully pimped her. Friends were falsely arrested, beaten up and wrongfully convicted. I sometimes used my little money to hire lawyers and cried often in court while the police laughed. I was shamed when they assumed I was a Triad girlfriend. When I had the privilege of visiting those sentenced to death or life imprisonment, I remembered my childhood question. It was both joy and weeping. It still is.

So now, because you asked, I must share a few of the hardest times. These are but representative and show, perhaps, where I was most vulnerable.

One day in a three-foot-wide lane dripping with whatever was leaked or poured out from above, I began to cry. I skidded past the overflowing, rat-infested sewer whilst on my way to a gray room where I held meetings that no one came to. *I could go back*, I thought, *to London, where they have civilized Bible studies and apologetics. Not all Christians live this way. But why, why on earth did I imply that it cost me nothing? It feels as though it costs everything.*

You see, just a few weeks before, I had been in a famous London church so crowded I had to sit on a stone sepulchre. I was introduced as "this wonderful girl who has given up everything to serve God in a poor place." I remember jumping off the grave and interrupting the speaker.

"No!" I exclaimed. "It cost nothing—I gained everything!"

Now, back in the dark slime, it felt as though it *did* cost everything. Why had I made such a proclamation? I had no perspective until a student from my prestigious school had an interpretation of my tongues. I did not understand all of her Cantonese, so I needed to look it up.

There is no one who has left house or brothers or sisters or father or mother or wife or children or lands, for My sake and the gospel's, who shall not receive a hundredfold now in this time— houses and brothers and sisters and mothers and children and lands, with persecutions—and in the age to come, eternal life.

Mark 10:29–30 NKJV

Yes, yes, yes! I not only get eternal life, but one hundred times what I left behind in this life! So I claimed, by faith, one hundred fathers, mothers, brothers, sisters, houses and lands in my lifetime, and supposed persecutions were part of the deal. Then I understood what I had proclaimed in London.

When you are wondering if you can pay the price, it seems as if you are giving up everything. When you have decided to pay it, you realize Jesus paid it all. It costs nothing. I was filled with His grace and love to go on. And I did. And He did, indeed, give me more than I asked. You can come to Hong Kong and see the hundreds and hundreds. Actually, thousands.

Almost a repeat version of that scenario occurred when my Walled City youth club was beaten up. Feces were smeared on the wall of the tiny room that I rented to give the youth and gangsters a chance at normal life. Ping-Pong, darts, Bible studies that no one attended, and an opportunity to join my summer camps, swimming, skate-boarding and hikes. I had opened it for all, and after spending years with them, was shattered to hear it was they who had smashed the windows and chairs and sullied the place with their betrayal.

I surveyed the debris.

"To him who strikes you on the one cheek, offer the other also" (Luke 6:29 NKJV).

Not sensible. But instead of clearing off to London's apologetics, I should stay.

Not sensible. They might do it again, or worse still, not come again.

"In everything give thanks" (1 Thessalonians 5:18 NKJV).

Not sensible. How to thank God for my friends beating up my place, which I had rented only for their good? Years of no dinner parties, no private life, all ending up in disgusting pooh. But there we were in the middle of a scenario that I sensed was the darkness before the dawn. I could go on.

So I cleaned the room up, and as I swept was muttering through tears, "Praise God! Praise God!" Because you should.

Not sensible. This was the moment of breakthrough. The gangster sent to guard me, after the massacre of my heart, had his own heart turned and changed. After some weeks of his watching and following me through the streets, he came into that room. He sang, he praised God, he prayed in tongues, came off opium miraculously and started a new life in Jesus.

His transformation was infectious. Triads and addicts queued up to meet the same Jesus. My house filled up, and some of my other Hong Kong friends joined in. Then followed years of learning. Instead of street ministry I was stuck in one apartment after another, trying to cope with the somewhat redeemed men who had started a new life but needed to grow up. I was not sure that the old things had passed away. Not all things seemed new.

Struggles and Healings

My hardest times have been with the "Church." I share this in the hope that it may encourage anyone experiencing the same struggles. I always had an instinct that I was supposed to be with the people of God, although I was not sent by, nor supported by, any particular group or denomination. I gathered, over the years, with many different kinds of believers, including those wonderful godly Plymouth Brethren who baptized me in water. I gathered with Spirit-filled Catholics, and with a house meeting full of believers from many denominations, all of whom wanted to learn about the baptism of the Holy Spirit and practice using the gifts of the Spirit to build each other up and reach the lost. We did.

There were often misunderstandings and misreports. Some of the little chapels I helped in were nervous about the sinners and gangsters I persuaded to come through their doors, and they disliked the clothes these visitors wore. The churchgoers wanted to change the sinners' hairstyles and shirts before recognizing their hearts.

An old Overseas Missionary Fellowship (OMF) missionary gave me some advice about that: "The church is not ready for them."

I was encouraged to grow them up secretly and safely as seedlings. This I did. And I kept away from the missionaries who were disturbed by the rumors of my being in nightclubs. *Better not stumble them*, I thought, and lay low.

171

When the numbers of drug addicts who wanted to know Jesus began to grow and grow, we discovered that all of them could receive the power of the Holy Spirit and the gift of tongues. They, like the first one, could come off drugs without pain or medication. My generous house church friends, Jean and Rick Willans, along with some others, helped finance, set up and look after more apartments for us, until they left Hong Kong.

Here, I cannot recount what ensued. Mostly due to lack of communication, everything fell apart, and I was left by myself again. I had written a successful book, but now there was nothing to show for all the years of miracles. Thanks to a visit to John Wimber in his early days, I got prayer. (The first time in sixteen years.) I did not know much how to receive prayer—I was so used to going it alone. But I was impressed by the persistence of John and his people, and by the way they cared for me. They prayed for me for a total of 29 hours in one week. I learned it was not a matter of who was right or wrong. I learned there was a need to address my hurts and perceptions, and to forgive, whether the offense was real or not. I got so healed and delivered that I rushed back to Hong Kong raring to go and a bit tender.

Tiredness and Weeping

I started again. More and more old Walled City boys and addicts came back, and my apartment filled up again. With no helpers, I did all the night duties, praying with people while half-sleeping on my knees by their bunk beds. Just as with the first men, I saw them freed as they prayed in tongues. But I had little sleep and no night clothes for years. My mother visited for the first time in seventeen years, and I was unable to take her out even for one meal. Men came and men left the house. Helpers came and helpers left. Much heartache and much weeping. Drugs in the house (they came in a box of egg tarts). Were these men really born again?

And then the visitors! Glorious bronzed Californians, surfers for Jesus and church planters. They looked at me and saw that I was exhausted and was often crying.

"Jackie," they said, "you're always crying and tired. Why don't you go off for a retreat with your helpers?"

I had neither permanent helpers, nor much physical rest. Who would look after the half-healed men when I went on retreat?

I learned to forgive them—those fired-up men with "visions." I felt much more tired after they left. There was much counsel, but they did not know how to love me by staying, learning the language and looking after our people so I *could* rest.

Poor Job! Afflictions must mean something is wrong. Poor Paul, beaten and shipwrecked yet again! He wrote,

> We are hard-pressed on every side, yet not crushed; we are perplexed, but not in despair; persecuted, but not forsaken; struck down, but not destroyed—always carrying about in the body the dying of the Lord Jesus, . . . that the life of Jesus also may be manifested in our mortal flesh. So then death is working in us, but life in you.
>
> 2 Corinthians 4:8–12 NKJV

This is the Gospel of Jesus. Christ chose to give up His life for me. He and the Father agreed on this. It brought death to the Giver and life to the receiver. He invites us to do the same. It was a privilege, not a punishment. My well-meaning visitors may not have been mature enough to remind me that my weakness could result in a manifestation of God's power. They did not know I was weeping not for myself, but for those who had gone astray.

173

Questions and Accusations

Lastly, though it was surely not the end of my conversation with the "Church," came a significant trial. Somehow, it seemed by mistake, we had exploded into a huge fellowship visited by thousands. We were living in a tin hut area, and our half-healed men and women were joined by many church leaders, who came to see what the Holy Spirit was doing in our Sunday afternoon meetings.

Some came in disguise and needed umbrellas, as the plastic roof leaked. Judges and policemen sat by street sleepers, and former addicts prayed over politicians. I separated men who were threatening each other with sharp meat cleavers before teaching on Leviticus. Lawyers were healed, and their children born again. A former prostitute stood tall in her white wedding garments, even though she was over sixty and under five feet. What joy and what fun!

"Are you a church or a fellowship?" came the question from visitors.

I could not be bothered with it, though it certainly bothered them.

"Do you think a woman should lead this church—what right have you?"

This was another one I could not relate to.

"How did you get all these numbers?" came from jealous church planters.

I had no idea, except that some of those I had looked after had grown up and won others, and we were a family. Over a hundred of us lived in this former squatter area as if it were heaven.

I saw our people and lived with them on Mondays, too. We were not a Sunday group, but cried and laughed daily. Sometimes there was much food, sometimes less. Sometimes much sleep, sometimes less. Still cockroaches and rats, but always worship and singing. We baptized many in a mildewed pool and longed to reach the world.

Most of the questions I could weather, by God's grace, until . . . the Big One.

One day, a couple came to my tin hut office. They had a list, I think it was 32 items of complaints against my leadership, and they said they represented the discontented foreign helpers. As they had not learned Cantonese, they probably had little idea what our local people felt. Later on, two other people repeated the complaints to me, so there was no mistake and no doubt about their grievances and criticisms.

I went down a deep hole. Did not know how to pray, but just cried instead. What is the point of confessing sins you do not know you have committed? But I did. Just in case.

I now lived outside the tin hut camp and crept in and out, hoping no one would notice me. If you have ever received an anonymous letter, you will know the feeling. Perhaps everyone thought I was a bad leader—they even accused me of being controlling. Was I? Were they right? I became totally nonfunctional for months and ran home to play solitaire or watch TV. The lost were still lost, but I was a bad leader. I tried not to catch anyone's eye in case they thought so, too. Nobody could fire me, though. I had not been hired!

An Act of Kindness

Eventually, I was rescued. A kind, kind man sat me down and spoke to me.

"Never mind," he said, "if they were right or wrong. What matters is your response to the situation."

It is our response to situations that shapes us. So he prayed with me and I confessed my feelings of hurt, quite apart from the validity of their complaints. I was healed. I was delivered. And I understood that opinions on leadership are not necessarily a matter of sin. I could have messed up, but I had done my best and I could go on.

"When He was reviled, [He] did not revile in return: when He suffered, He did not threaten, but committed Himself to Him who judges righteously" (1 Peter 2:23 NKJV).

I could gladly forgive my accusers; I am sure they meant good. God certainly did.

Most of all, I am thankful for that kind man who loved me enough to point out where the real problem lay, and see me freed from the grip the enemy had over me so I could go on in God's grace.

> But in all things approving ourselves as the ministers of God, in much patience, in afflictions, in necessities, in distresses, in stripes, in imprisonments, in tumults, in labours, in watchings, in fastings; by pureness, by knowledge, by long suffering, by kindness, by the Holy Ghost, by love unfeigned, by the word of truth, by the power of God, by the armour of righteousness on the right hand and on the left, by honour and dishonour, by evil report and good report: as deceivers, and yet true; as unknown, and yet well known; as dying, and, behold, we live; as chastened, and not killed; as sorrowful, yet alway rejoicing; as poor, yet making many rich; as having nothing, and yet possessing all things.
>
> 2 Corinthians 6:4–10 KJV

This is just part of my life story. How my heart was captured by Jesus, who privileged me to take God's love into one of the darkest places on earth and who met me in my darkest times. He walked with me in them and stunningly turned them into opportunities for His light and love to break through. I am *almost* looking forward to the hard times ahead!

The light shines in the darkness,
Jackie Pullinger

Jackie Pullinger has lived in Hong Kong since 1966. St. Stephen's Society grew out of her ongoing passion to preach the Gospel, reach the poor and see people set free through faith in Jesus Christ. Information about her people's lives and ongoing stories is available at http://www.ststephenssociety.com.

12

Expecting Nothing in Return

By James W. Goll

But now faith, hope and love abide, these three; but
the greatest of these is love.

1 Corinthians 13:13 NASB

This is James Goll, residing in Pleasantville, U.S.A., otherwise known as Franklin, Tennessee. I grew up in a small rural community in Missouri called Cowgill, with a population of 259 people, possibly counting the cows and chickens. Unlike most, I do not remember a B.C. (Before Christ). All I have ever known is Jesus. He has been my best friend every day of my life, and I will close out my days on this side with Jesus as my best friend and older brother.

I have already lived an amazing life in Christ. I love the love of God! I am an addict. The majestic attributes of God and the overwhelming beauty of the Lord Jesus Christ amaze me. The wonder of the ever-present Holy Spirit captures me again and again. I love knowing God. I love *loving* God. I love how He so perfectly loves you and me.

Both Sides Now

Then I encountered my dear Jesus in another way. I was graced by gifts of the Holy Spirit during the charismatic era of the 1970s, and I was eventually propelled as a pioneer into the global prayer and prophetic movements. I heard the external, audible voice of the Lord telling me whom to marry, Michal Ann Willard. I married her, the girl of my dreams, on the exact date the Holy Spirit told me. We brought forth miracle children when it was impossible for us to conceive. Together we had angelic visitations lasting for nine straight weeks.

I have traveled as an ambassador for the sake of Christ in more than fifty nations. I have seen thousands of Jewish people in the former Soviet Union place their faith in Jesus as their Messiah. I saw, and declared prophetically, that the walls of Communism would come down—long before they actually did. I have witnessed blind eyes seeing, tumors dissolving, demons fleeing, leaders being reconciled and apostolic movements being birthed. I know there are many more demonstrations of God's great grace still to come.

And I got to watch those four bona fide, medically documented miracles grow up right in my own home. They are all married adults today, good-looking and smart, highly favored, diverse, unique and creatively gifted. Each of them loves God. I am a proud father and grandfather.

This does not mean I did not experience some intense times and long days, wondering when the sun was going to pierce through the darkness. I have known times of abundance and years of leanness. In fact, in the last few years of my life, it seemed as if I have suffered from identity theft or have exchanged IDs with someone else. Pinnacles to pits. Peaks to valleys. High places to low places. From life's journey, I look at life from both sides now. I now have some understanding of the complexity and oddity of the writings contained in the book of Ecclesiastes:

> There is an appointed time for everything. And there is a time for every event under heaven—a time to give birth and a time to die; a time to plant and a time to uproot what is planted. A time to kill and a time to heal; a time to tear down and a time to build up. A time to weep and a time to laugh; a time to mourn and a time to dance.
>
> Ecclesiastes 3:1–4 NASB

I have had the honor of composing more than thirty books thus far. I did not choose writing; it seems as if it chose me. But what I am about to pen is the most transparent and earthly dramatization by far. It might also be the hardest.

Early Beginnings

My dear dad was kicked out of his home when he was twelve years old, the oldest of seven siblings. He raised himself during the Great Depression, was homeless for a season and received only a sixth-grade education. My muscular dad—hardworking, once very good-looking, with dazzling bright blue eyes—did not know how to receive or give love. I weep as I think about how God softened this verbally abusive man's heart later in life. I was eventually honored to lead my daddy into the waters of baptism as he rededicated his life to Jesus, and I even preached a message on grace at his funeral. But most of my life, I lived in fear of this tough, once "not safe" man known by many simply as Wayne.

My persevering mom came from the other side of the tracks. She was raised by holiness parents, dedicated to Christ at an early age and taught to love the church. She was college educated, sensitive and prayerful. Beautiful Amanda Elizabeth Burns had an hourglass figure when she married Kenneth Wayne Goll during the height of World War II.

My parents were opposites for sure, and the incongruity often showed up with verbal intensity and relational dysfunction in our home as they attempted to rear their three children in rural Missouri. We were poor. Mom gardened and made quilts. But in the midst of it all, they taught us to do what was right and care for others. I learned forgiveness from observing my mom.

I grew up the youngest of three siblings and a bit fragile. I was wired as ultrasensitive, I had a fear-filled rejection complex and I was probably a bit "otherly." I talked to the clouds and the ants in our front yard as though they were my friends. I walked the railroad tracks for hours and talked to God, and I thought He talked back. After all, isn't that what those hymns taught that we bellowed out at the Methodist church? "And He walks with me, and He talks with me, and He tells me I am His own. . . ."

Yes, I was pierced by the enchanting lyrics of the hymn "I Come to the Garden Alone" (also known as "In the Garden," C. Austin Miles). Those words still pierce me today. In my heart there still rings a melody. If I die before the Second Coming of Christ, I want hymns sung at my memorial service.

But while growing up, I never seemed to fit in anywhere. I won some math and science awards at Braymer High School and was gearing up to be a world-famous engineer in space development. But high school was like living torture. I lived the song "Cry Me a River," crying myself to sleep most nights. As a sophomore, I actually asked the Lord to take me home.

I knew the Lord Jesus, though, and He restrained me from doing what a lot of the other teenagers did. And when I sang,

I felt celebrated. So sing I did. I sang on long walks. I sang at church and at school. I sang in choirs, madrigals and solos at music contests, where I won awards. I sang in college. I arranged and directed the music for a choral group called The Seekers, and I was a smooth-crooning baritone in a contemporary Jesus trio called Light of the Day. I always sang loudly, too. (Ha! I was told the other day that I still sing loudly.)

Why did I sing? "I sing because I'm happy, I sing because I'm free, for His eye is on the sparrow, and I know He watches me" (from the hymn "His Eye Is on the Sparrow," lyrics Civilla D. Martin, music Charles H. Gabriel). I sang because it seemed to please Jesus. I sang because my daddy's eyes would glisten when I sang. He loved me when I sang.

My wife and I received a framed calligraphy print as a wedding present on May 15, 1976. It reads, *God respects me when I work. But He loves me when I sing.* This print has hung over every bedroom doorway we (now I) have ever had.

Someday I might just sprout wings and fly away. When I do, I will do it with a song in my heart and lyrics resounding across the skies. "This is my story, this is my song, praising my Savior all the day long; this is my story, this is my song, praising my Savior all the day long" (from "Blessed Assurance," lyrics Fanny Crosby, music Phoebe Knapp). It is not just singing I love; it is worshiping!

Who Turned On the Lights?

After high school, while attending Central Missouri State University, my life took a dramatic turn: I ran smack-dab into the Jesus people. For a skinny kid and rural Methodist, this was a paradigm shift. Long-haired, hippie-looking creatures wearing bell-bottoms played guitars and jammed offbeat with tambourines. They talked to me incessantly about Jesus, as though they really knew Him, and about the baptism in the Holy Spirit. For the longest time, it all sounded like a bunch of mumbo jumbo. Then, the summer I turned twenty, I attended Explo '72 at the Cotton Bowl in Dallas. On the fifth night of the rally, Billy Graham spoke a piercing message on commitment. I stood obediently to my feet on that humid, sacred night, with no emotions stirring whatsoever, and consecrated myself to be some kind of minister of the Gospel.

It was over! My plans to be a NASA engineer were now doomed. I set my hand zealously to the plow of God's work and have never looked back.

Then, during Thanksgiving break of my junior year of college, I received by faith the baptism in the Holy Spirit. I started prophesying immediately and have never quit. My little black-and-white inner TV screen turned into OmniVision overnight, and I started having internal mental pictures and intrusions of inspired thought patterns. Later I came to understand that these were visions and the gift of the word of knowledge.

Now I have enjoyed more than 42 years of hearing from the Holy Spirit and releasing His gifts. He wrecked me, and He keeps playing havoc with my life to this day!

I graduated from Central Missouri State with a degree in social work. But my real schooling and job description were being a Jesus freak. I prayer-walked, fasted, witnessed in bars, mentored others, practiced casting out demons, worshiped and prophesied. Unofficially, then, I majored in hearing God's voice and prayer. I loved my new education. I take classes from the Holy Spirit to this day, and I recommend that you do, too.

Who Turned Off the Lights?

Let me fast-forward this story line. I "married up" to an angel, and we sang beautifully together. And after our four miracle kids, more prayer and fasting, journeys into missions and much more, I gave up pastoring and joined an emerging ragtag team of leaders called the Kansas City Prophets. We wanted to change the understanding and expression of Christianity across the face of the earth. It was awesome—glorious, experimental and very costly.

The resilient Mike Bickle pioneered the way, while international leaders across the Body of Christ came gazing into the public goldfish bowl of the Kansas City Fellowship. Then a hellish global spiritual warfare controversy broke out concerning the prophetic. Through my relationships with the Kansas City Prophets, I was caught in the middle of the firestorm. Hurt. Pain. Misunderstanding. Anguish. My anger turned to internal rage over the loss of many friendships and associations. We were called heretics, lunatics and anything else with a *tic*—so it seemed. Once we could do nothing wrong, and now we seemingly could do nothing right.

From being bright lights in the Kingdom of God to being treated as if we were a cult was one hard pill to swallow. I will always be grateful, though, for the historic opportunity to change history in the Body of Christ. Today a lot of what the Kansas City Prophets pioneered is accepted as everyday, common understanding in many circles of the Church.

Michal Ann and I moved our family and ministry base to the greater Nashville area, and all seemed great for a while. I taught for three straight years on Monday nights and was able to influence many who are mature leaders today in the Body of Christ.

Then it was as if the hordes of hell were released again. I was hit with three different battles with non-Hodgkin's lymphoma cancer over more than eight years. I sought healing, took Communion daily, declared the Scriptures, called the elders of the city to pray and trusted God. Ultimately, I had a visitation with the Man of Fire, Jesus. Perseverance had its reward, and I have been clean and clear of cancer for more than five years now. It is never coming back!

But while I was battling, Michal Ann faced her own fight for her life against the ugly progression of colon cancer. No one ever fought harder than this dear woman, seeking out healing in every disciplined, holistic and scriptural manner. She had six organs cut out of her body, and eventually she had an ostomy bag and had two brain tumors removed. She still traveled the globe and launched her ministry called Compassion Acts while racked with pain, with two ribs broken due to tumorous growths. But she was cheerful all the way and changed lives for Jesus' sake. Everyone loved Annie.

Every morning this woman on the frontlines would wake up with a smile on her face, feeling her body to see if her new body parts had shown up yet. Eventually, on September 15, 2008, dear Annie sprouted wings and flew away to worship the Lover of her soul. I hear heavenly reports from time to time that she is doing well, dancing with her first Boyfriend and dressed in a wedding garment made out of diamonds.

We endured the loss of hundreds of thousands of dollars due to medical bills. We lost 70 percent of our donor base because they did not know how to respond to our dark night. We found ourselves surrounded by some of Job's friends who had aligned themselves with the accuser of the brethren. People thought we had to be in sin. I was accused of everything from homosexuality, immorality, pornography and theft to being a control freak.

Did I walk perfectly? No. But Michal Ann knew a kind of selfless love. She had been praying for me for years, that I would not be enamored of gifted people or large gifts, but that I would earnestly desire spiritual gifts while letting love be my aim (as Paul exhorted in 1 Corinthians 14:1). Now I began to learn to love in a whole different dimension, and to forgive and bless every step of the way. I learned to interpret people's views in a redemptive manner.

Some people came up with simple, pat answers as to why these terrible things were happening to Michal Ann and me. They just wanted things fixed; they wanted *us* fixed. And actually, in their own way, they were attempting to express concern and love toward us. Although I had to put most of their lotions and potions, pills and oils, suggestions and words on the shelf, I did learn to receive these unrequested intrusions as feeble acts of love. They cared.

Touched by a Love I Never Knew

Dealing with our health battles and people's responses was hard. But let me tell you the hardest and best lesson I learned in this new walk of unconditional love. In May 2008, I was leading a prayer tour in Israel and participating in The Call Jerusalem. Toward the end of the tour, I sensed from the Holy Spirit that I was to return home three days early and leave the remaining portion of the tour in others' capable hands. I knew that a healing was going to happen upon my arrival. So in agreement with the team, I changed my ticket and flew home three days early.

When I arrived at our beautiful farmhouse in Franklin, Tennessee, I turned to the full-time live-in helper we had hired for Michal Ann and gave her the weekend off. I would take care of my Annie myself.

But Michal Ann had just completed another round of chemotherapy and was reacting violently to the treatment. Early the next morning, she got out of bed and ran into the bathroom, confused. She began to heave, actually broke a blood vessel in her brain, and started spitting up red, green and ugly stuff. She was not fully "present."

Standing stark naked in the bathroom, with vomit all over her once-beautiful body, she took out the clip holding her ostomy bag in place. Things went from bad to horrific. Bad-smelling excrement flowed all over her and all over the bathroom floor.

I tried the best I could to clean her up. I walked her into the bedroom and sat her on the bed. Then I returned to the bathroom, where I knelt down on my hands and knees to clean up the mess on the floor. I was gagging and about to throw up myself. I was also weeping. No—I was sobbing convulsively.

Annie, back to herself, heard my moaning and groaning and thought I had fallen or had hurt myself.

With concern and love, she called, "Jim, are you hurting? Are you in pain or something?"

While I was on my knees on the bathroom floor, about to puke, her words pierced me. I thought, *Am I hurting? Am I in pain or something? How do I answer that?*

Then, as I was on my knees, the invisible finger of God came and touched me. The Holy Spirit went into the deepest place of my heart and gave me a love I had never known. I felt it. I knew it. That hard morning, at my very darkest moment, the finger of God touched me and gave me a love that expects nothing in return.

For six months I had been crying out to the Lord privately, telling Him I was at the end of my own love. The circumstances of our ordeal had taken their toll on me. I was still in my own fight with cancer, and now my amazing, compassionate lady was ravaged by the horrors of cancer, multiple surgeries and the effects of all the various treatments.

I did not know how to love my dearest wife and closest friend, Annie, anymore. I was empty. I was past my own love.

That day, a miracle happened. A healing occurred. Not the one I was expecting or longing for. It was the one Michal Ann had been praying for me to experience for years—that I would let love be my aim, even while earnestly desiring the spiritual gifts. She had had it right. At times I had had it in reverse. But a room opened up in my heart—a room for which I now have the key. A room I can still enter into.

For the following four months, I walked in a love I had never known. I held Annie, gently swayed in dance with her, sat in rocking chairs on the southern front porch and said nothing, but watched the hummingbirds and drank organic green tea with her. I learned to love, expecting nothing in return.

Annie's prayers were answered. Perhaps one of her major assignments in life was complete. She had passed the love test and was released to fly away. She had lived a life of love. Now it was my turn to experience and answer the question that the Lord asked Bob Jones, as we heard in the first chapter of this raw book: *Did you learn how to love?*

I am sobbing again as I pen this in transparency. I am weeping in gratitude that I have been granted another opportunity in life to learn to love.

So here you are. I just opened up my treasure chest to bring out one of my most prized possessions: a love that expects nothing in return.

Sometimes I still face things that are hard. Sometimes I forget that room.

Then the Holy Spirit nudges me and reminds me, *I gave you a key to a room. Just put the key into the door and walk back into that chamber of My heart in your heart. There abide faith, hope and love. And the greatest of these is love.*

Here it is in Scripture:

Love is patient, love is kind and is not jealous; love does not brag and is not arrogant, does not act unbecomingly; it does not seek its own, is not provoked, does not take into account a wrong suffered, does not rejoice in unrighteousness, but rejoices with the truth; bears all things, believes all things, hopes all things, endures all things.

Love never fails; but if there are gifts of prophecy, they will be done away; if there are tongues, they will cease; if there is knowledge, it will be done away. For we know in part and we prophesy in part; but when the perfect comes, the partial will be done away. When I was a child, I used to speak like a child, think like a child, reason like a child; when I became a man, I did away with childish things. For now we see in a mirror dimly, but then face to face; now I know in part, but then I will know fully just as I also have been fully known. But now faith, hope, love, abide these three; but the greatest of these is love.

1 Corinthians 13:4–13 NASB

This, then, is what love looks like to me. I have a key to a room in God's heart.

In this book, some of my friends have shared part of their stories. Each of us has a story. You do, too. And you have a personal God just waiting to teach you His ways. You, too, can receive a key to life lived from the heart. Take that key!

Because love never fails.

Let This Be Our Prayer

As we come to the end of these amazing stories about what love looks like and as we close out these pages together, let this be our prayer:

Father, in the wonderful name of Jesus, we come to You right now. We humble our minds in pure worship and bow in our hearts to the only One who is worthy. We ask that You grant each of us a fresh measure of Your divine love that expects nothing in return. Teach us to love. Work in our lives so that others will truly see "what love looks like." May the world know that we are Your disciples by the love we have for one another, for mankind and for our most gracious God. Thank You for being such a great Mentor and a brilliant Teacher. And lead us into the path less traveled. Teach us how to love.

With deep sincerity,
James W. Goll

James W. Goll is president of Encounters Network, international director of Prayer Storm and founder of God Encounters Training, an e-school of the heart. His wife, Michal Ann, was founder of Compassion Acts. Information about his ministries is available at http://www.encountersnetwork.com.

More from James W. Goll

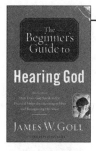

The God of the universe wants to speak to *you*. Are you ready to receive His words? Will you understand what He says? This hands-on guide lays out clear biblical principles for listening to God, offering real-life examples and practical methods for hearing God when He speaks.

The Beginner's Guide to Hearing God

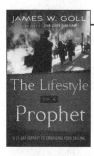

Journey into the heart of the prophetic calling! This unique 21-day guide will help you develop the intimacy with God essential to hearing His voice clearly. Reflection questions and practical applications will help you proclaim His words faithfully—and step boldly into your calling.

The Lifestyle of a Prophet

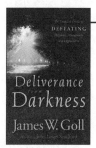

James Goll offers his wisdom and insight in one straightforward, action-oriented manual on the topic of deliverance. With a range of step-by-step solutions, you can start defeating demonic strongholds and oppression, and break free from the bonds of darkness today.

Deliverance from Darkness

✓Chosen

Stay up-to-date on your favorite books and authors with our free e-newsletters. Sign up today at chosenbooks.com.

Find us on Facebook. facebook.com/chosenbooks

Follow us on Twitter. @chosenbooks